Better Health with Culinary Herbs

Other Books
EAT THE WEEDS
KITCHEN MEDICINES

BEN CHARLES HARRIS

Better Health
with
Culinary
Herbs

Weathervane Books
New York

Acknowledgments

Among the many who have made helpful suggestions, and inspired many of the ideas and recipes which appear in this book, I would especially like to thank Beatrice Trum Hunter, author of *The Organic Foods Cook Book;* The Herb Society of America, which publishes *Flavors And Savors;* the members of my herb study classes; the American Spice Trade Association, which publishes *Spice of Life;* the California Wine Advisory Board; Lewis Hodgkinson. of the Worcester County Extension Service and Paul Rogers of Stonehedge Herb Gardens.

Dedication

To the loving memory of my father,
whose motto for successful living was:

"Cooperation with others,
Sincerity of one's self."

Contents

I

Culinary Herbs

1

Herbs for Flavor and Fitness

A precise definition of an herb is elusive. One man's herb, especially in our day, is another man's weed. Oliver Wendell Holmes
once defined a weed as any plant whose medicinal benefits have
not yet been discovered. Such a discovery of economic value—as
food, as medicine or for other uses—would elevate the formerly
lowly plant to the status of an herb. Herbs have an ancient history, perhaps as old as that of man himself; they have been used
as food, as seasoning in the preparation of food, as specific remedies for a variety of ailments, as dyes, as scents and as cosmetics.
These benefits are not exclusive, and the user of a single herb may
at one sitting be deriving important nutrients, enhancing the
flavor of the food he is eating and counteracting an unhealthy
condition he might happen to have.

Culinary herbs are different from spices, which appear to have
similar uses. The word culinary (pronounced kew-linary) is derived from the Latin *culina,* meaning kitchen, and refers to cooking. Any portion of a plant, fruit or vegetable—roots, stems,
leaves or seeds—possessing savory qualities produced by its aromatic oils may be used as a culinary herb, to season or flavor
foods.*

* Certain herbs should be eaten fresh in order to obtain their full nutritional value. Chervil, chives, parsley, nasturtium and watercress, to mention
a few herbs, add extra zest and taste appeal to salads, and will provide their

There are two basic reasons why you would and should use culinary herbs: to enhance the flavor of foods and to directly contribute to your health.

Economy appeals to everyone, especially in these days of inflation. One way to be economical, with a gourmet touch, is to perk up leftovers with culinary herbs. Homemakers should review the lessons they learned during World War II, and treat herbs as a budget aid. Today, most stores carry as many as 60 seasoning herbs and spices, and since 1930, it has been estimated that the per capita use of the herbs alone has increased approximately 25%. This growth, said one journal, was due to American tourists who returned from abroad with exotic recipes; but the herbalist and herb grower aver that the increase was the result of the war-time necessity which taught housewives to be bolder in their flavoring of bland and monotonous meals and to vary the familiar dishes—especially leftovers. Many herb bulletins of State Extension Services will attest to this fact.

The past 20 years have taught the American homemaker more about the art of cooking and the need of properly preparing meals than any comparable period in our history, and have caused a great change in our food habits and preferences. While food rationing in the war time taught most homemakers important lessons in better nutrition and food utilization, it also emphasized to a large degree the need of improving the flavor of everyday foods, leftovers and quick pickup meals with basil, marjoram or savory. These herbs worked wonders with inexpensive cuts of meat and lent their subtle flavors to leftover hamburger or meat loaf, vegetable soup or stew. A cornucopia of vitamins and minerals abound in such lower-priced health sustainers as the humble potato, cheeses, and cabbage. Such simple foods as cabbage and lettuce soon acquire glamor in a Caesar or chef's salad enlivened by a few drops of home-made garlic or tarragon

optimum nutritional benefits only if they are eaten uncooked, for heat only destroys their nutrients.

vinegar, and cheese hors d'oeuvres are far more interesting with a tiny sprinkle of basil or marjoram. In time, with sufficient patience and experimentation, the art of cooking with herbs will be acquired by the resourceful cook.

Cooks who never use herbs except for a little thyme or sage in poultry stuffing have discovered, much to their surprise and pleasure, that seasonings with other meats are equally desirable. The tougher cuts of meat derive a delightful lift from a pinch of rosemary or basil.

The culinaries are often taken for granted. I have found that until many cooks have been taught the reasons for seasoning their food with herbs, they will continue to use the harsh, irritating spices. But when they realize the multiple benefits derived from the use of herbs they will call the freshly cut herb, "friend of the physician and the praise of cooks." Herb seasoning may be desirable every day of the year, but not everything we eat must be herb seasoned. Herbs will not overcome or correct faulty eating habits and other everyday sins; neither will they undo the havoc resulting from the consumption of nutritionless but well advertised man-made food substitutes. To truly appreciate the value of herbs, do not use them in every meal, in too many dishes. Most people who enjoy the savory properties of herbs know little of the health-insuring properties of the thyme or marjoram that makes dinner a highlight of the day. The former eater of excessively fatty meats and fish, fried, greasy foods and beef stews, and the like, was often afflicted by after-dinner nausea, heartburn or indigestion. His dinner required the inevitable "chaser" of Tums or Alka Seltzer and frequent and hurried visits to the doctors and drug-stores. But once culinaries were added to his soup or fish, he found that the very fragrance of the herb, however faint, successfully encouraged his taste glands when previously eating had been a dreaded chore and a profuse supply of stimulants (liquor and medicine) had been needed to "force" an appetite. These stimulants are easily avoided and needless. A pinch of dill or marjoram, for example, on baked fish eliminates the inevitable post-meal discomfort due to the indigestible fish oil.

So there is more to the gentle seasoners than meets the culinary tongue. Flavor is one aspect: even simple meals are made epicurean by the wise and frequent use of aromatic herbs. Savory herbs do create mystery and glamor in innumerable cooking recipes, especially of the French and Italian variety. They animate the too often over-cooked protein foods. But it is equally true that culinaries offer excellent service by insuring the more complete assimilation of food nutriments. The all-important factor which applies to herbs, culinary or medicinal, is the power of most aromatic and savory herbs to prevent disease at the source.

The major purpose of such essentials as sage, marjoram, and savory in a given recipe is to act as preventive medicines. Carrots, celery, parsley and other vegetables and fruits, when eaten uncooked, protect the human system from premature decay and disease, by furnishing needed minerals and vitamins. The medical profession agrees that most of our everyday ailments arise from irregularities of the stomach and intestines, specifically from catarrhal formations (irritations or inflammations) along the delicate mucous lining of the alimentary system, from the esophagus to and including the lower intestines. The toxic catarrh, often the principal cause of asthma or bronchitis, etc., is the result of having eaten daily doses of greasy, fried foods, of super-boiled soups and stews; and gray, chlorophyll-less (and therefore nutritionless) vegetables, coarse meats that are supersaturated with artery-hardening cholesterol and gravy. The use of culinary herbs frequently prevents the already formed catarrh from over-staying its unwelcome visit. The causes of organic disorders (excessive cholesterol and catarrh and faulty dietary habits in general) may be removed and the body may soon revitalize itself.

No doubt the cook who is forever frying foods is not repulsed by the fat or grease that has recently congealed in her frying pan. Here is a prime cause of digestive trouble and lowered vitality. Such foods may hinder the proper functions of the body's organs and lead to illness—chronic constipation, kidney and gall bladder disorders, colitis, and arthritis. Following each fried meal, Ajax or Babo is needed to clean the greasy frying pan. The cooks devoted to the frying pan will also periodically require the services of cans of lye to clear the drain pipes of their kitchen sinks which have become clogged with fatty refuse. In a crude sense, there is an analogy between the use of culinary herbs to season foods and the use of soap and hot water to dissolve the recently congealed fat or butter of the frying pan. The "pipes" of the human alimentary system, like those of the sink, often become clogged with dangerous catarrhal formations. Culinary herbs are alkaline in action and reaction, aromatic and warming to the taste, and when ingested with foods generally act as a mild diaphoretic (to cause gentle perspiration) and as a carminative (to expel and prevent gas) and thus relieve colic and prevent colitis and other disturbances. The herb's alkaline salts combine with its aromatic principles or volatile oils and work to counteract the fat or catarrhal-forming principles of many foods.

You may have heard the oft-repeated saws: "You dig your grave with your teeth" and "A man is as old as his arteries; as strong as his heart (or blood stream)." There is an important connection between these two sayings. The fact that unneeded fat tissue makes the heart strain to pump blood to the blood vessels is recognized by the medical profession as a contributing factor in various cardio-vascular diseases. Running a close second to America's number one killer, coronary (heart) disease, is arteriosclerosis, a disease commonly identified as "hardening of the arteries." The victim of either of these coronary ills has contributed to his own condition by long-established dietary faults which include needless overeating of fatty meats, fried foods, pastries and other conventional foods. The cholesterol contained in meat fats is deposited along the inner walls of the coronary artery that channels the blood to the heart; this narrows and

hardens the inner walls of the artery, forcing the heart to over-
work, and often resulting in heart failure. Diabetics should
sharply reduce their intake of cholesterol because they are more
susceptible to the hardening of the arterial system than the non-
diabetics. It would be presumptuous to say that marjoram and
sage or other culinary herbs alone may prevent coronary derange-
ments. But the aromatic and alkaline properties of culinary
herbs may prevent catarrhal formations along the alimentary
system.

Many of the fresh green vegetables contain two valuable substances called inositol and choline, which are members of the
B Complex group, and help to lower the vicious cholesterol
content in the bloodstream. One should always remember that
besides being careful about what one eats, one should also be
concerned about how much one eats. Of the many dietary faults,
overeating is the one fault most to avoid. The fat man is supposed
to be a jolly fellow but he is also most susceptible to arterial and
coronary disorders. Do use herbs in cooking or as a tea or coffee
substitute, but do not be misled. They are not a cure-all.

Here are several examples which demonstrate the dual benefits of culinary herbs:

Fennel is a must whenever fish is served so that the rather
indigestible, fatty oil may be properly counter-balanced by the
carminative, aromatic properties of the herb. Herbalists, centuries ago, knew of its properties. As Culpepper aptly put it:
"One goode old custom is not yet left off, viz., to boil fennel
with fish, for it consumes the phlegmatic humors which fish most
plentifully afford and annoy the body with, though few that use
it know wherefore they do it."

Herbalist John Parkinson advocated the necessity of seasoning foods with herbs to prevent unforeseen illnesses. Parkinson
said, "Marjoram herbe is used in meates and brothes to helpe a
cold Stomacke and to expel wind."

The reason for including summer savory in any recipe is basi-
cally a matter of preventing serious organic ailments. The beneficial essence of its aromatic volatile oil tends to correct and

prevent a possible dangerous catarrhal condition in the intestines known as colitis and other inflammatory conditions. "Summer Savory is both sharpe and quicke in taste, expelling winde in the stomacke and bowels." The alkalizing principles of this herb help to prevent the artery-hardening cholesterol from causing too much damage to the blood stream.

John Parkinson said of thyme ". . . Besides the physicall uses to many purposes for the head, stomacke, spleen, etc., there is no herb almost of more use, . . . both for inward and outward occasions; . . . inwardly in most sorts of broths, with Rosemary, and to make sawce for divers sorts of both fish and fleshe, as to stuffe the belly of a goose to bee rosted and after put into the sawce, on meates when it is rosted, or fried fish." But Parkinson had noted well thyme's ever important healing property in bronchitis, whooping cough and similar ailments, declaring that it "hath the power to drive forthe flegme." This property is indeed corroborated by the conservative United States Dispensatory. Bronchial catarrh is caused by the accumulation of phlegm along the linings of the bronchia, and the use of thyme with fatty foods may prevent its formation.

By the same token the cook will discover that many if not most mouth-watering herbal seasoners such as sage, anise, basil, among others, offer time-tested medicinal and therapeutic properties. A warm tea of mixed anise and caraway seeds and catnip will serve as an equally effective anti-colic remedy or carminative for a six-month-old infant or for his sixty-year-old grandfather. A simple effective cough remedy is prepared by drinking teas of anise and thyme, in which solution horehound and garden hollyhock roots have been previously boiled.

Need a soothing eye lotion? See the formula under fennel, to which may be added the common chamomile and uncommon eyebright.

For measles, have the patient drink warm teas made of equal parts catnip and marjoram plus a pinch of saffron, and the patient will quickly recover, with far less eruptive itchings than usual.

Under tisanes, I have offered a few examples of herb teas and their medicinal uses. Tisanes, aromatically pleasing and healthy, illustrate the theme of flavor and fitness. A certain men's club in New York City, I am told, serves the members not alcoholic liquors but an herb tea somewhat similar to my "Northern Julep." The herbs for the club's tisane were three: peppermint, sage, and lemon verbena. Several exclusive beauty salons (also in New York) serve warm chamomile tea to soothe the nerves and tempers of their patrons as they while away their waiting time.

In the past dozen years or so, herb cookery and herb recipes have become a necessity. Herb mills and seed grinders are fast becoming kitchen accessories. The consumer, shopping around for unusual culinary delights, has at long last become more aware of the dozens of herbal seasoners. These herbs, now grown scientifically and expertly dried, are packaged in various attractive ways—in fancy racks, in fancier bottles and apothecary jars, and in plain glassine bags. Today, many stores sell these herbed items: salad dressings or the herb mixture for that preparation, herbed wines and vinegars, herb tea mixtures (tisanes), herb sauces and spreads, herb jellies and preserves and herb salt substitutes. There are also "herbal" cosmetics and shampoos.

2

Sugar and Spice and Everything Salted

Ginger and mustard are often improperly placed in the same class as culinary herbs, but these two, as others like them, should be called condiments, from the Latin *condimentum,* meaning spice. They are generously employed in commercial vinegars, curry powders, mustard and other harsh sauces, mixed pickle relishes and catsups, and together with the other spices, are not recommended as seasoning agents. A partial list of spices would contain: allspice, cinnamon, cloves, ginger, mace, mustard, nutmeg, paprika, black, white and red pepper, turmeric, chili powder, curry powder and pickling mixtures.

It is a known fact that the frequent use of such stimulants as mustard, pepper and vinegar unbalances the digestive juices and irritates the delicate stomach lining, often leading to intestinal catarrh, and later, ulcers. The use of improper seasonings creates just the opposite of what is intended. This is best known by those who habitually eat in restaurants,* where at arm's reach there is usually a variety of harsh seasonings and relishes, which are needed to resurrect the savor of over-cooked, tasteless foods.

The longer you heat your foods, the more nutrients you are

---

* Nothing so exasperates a careful cook as to see a diner take a salt shaker in one hand, a pepper box in the other, and sprinkle their contents over the dish he has prepared, without even trying to find out whether he had properly seasoned it in the kitchen.

destroying. Spices are usually added to foods which have been cooked or *boiled until spoiled*. Such meals are at best barely nourishing, lifeless and tasteless. The addition of condiments to unappetizing fare becomes an unfortunate and unhealthy necessity. Physicians have long observed that in tropical countries where curry and related condiments are extensively used, diseases of the liver and stomach are exceedingly common. I heard of a man who returned from his travels in Mexico and described a favorite native dish as composed of layers of the following ingredients: "Pepper, mustard, ginger; pepper, potatoes, ginger; mustard, pepper, potatoes; mustard, ginger, pepper." That compares almost as well with the flavor imagination of many a housewife: salt, vinegar, mustard, pepper—over and over again. These spices are not recommended as seasoning agents. They upset, rather than aid, digestion by over-stimulating the stomach juices and eventually causing the digestive apparatus to become weakened. Most condiments and spices lack any food value and once ingested they usually tend to irritate the digestive tract and the blood vessels. Experiments with animals, described by Arnold DeVries in *The Fountain of Youth*, have shown that the daily use of mustard will "cause blood vessels to harden and thicken to protect themselves against the spice; while pepper produced a shortened life span, hardening of the liver, congestion of the kidney and gradual degeneration of cells." Mustard, pepper and ginger can be applied to the skin to produce a warming sensation. They are employed as medications, for example, in mustard plasters, embrocations of pepper and lard, and liniments, but the use of such stimulants should be confined to external purposes, such as described in my book, *Kitchen Medicines*.

The addition of salt and condiments to any prepared food is a gastronomic sin. Today, they are on the physician's taboo list. Commercially prepared relishes and pickles offer a minimum of nutrients. They are worthless, a needless expense, and more often than not give rise to serious and costly gastric disturbances. These items must be avoided by all who suffer with kidney disorders, high blood pressure, obesity, and other conventional discomforts. Ask anyone having these difficulties who has recently seen the doctor, what kind of a diet must be followed, and invariably the answer will be low fat, salt free and spice free. The dietary regimen is the same, no matter what the ailment—arthritis, diabetes, colitis, to name a few.

The dangers of using salt as seasoning for table use should be emphasized. It is a dangerous chemical without which the human body can do very well. The contention that salt, the commercial product, sodium chloride, improves digestion is open to serious debate. This chemical is not only unsuitable for the human body; it interferes with normal digestion of foods by decreasing by one-third to one-half the protein-digesting action of the enzyme pepsin.

The use of the chemical as a seasoner at meal time can lead only to serious organic ailments. It is little wonder then, that millions of Americans are now and ever on a salt-free diet. Once they ate meals dosed with this toxic chemical, and suffered the torments and the aches and pains of their respective ailments, be it heart trouble, high blood pressure, obesity, nephritis, diabetes or arthritis.

Salt, as a seasoning agent or medicine, is forbidden by the medical profession to persons suffering from arteriosclerosis or hardening of the arteries, gout and rheumatism, edema and dropsy, cirrhosis of the liver, Bright's disease or other kidney disorders, hyperacidity and gastric ulcer. In addition, medical opinion has suggested that salt tends to cause constipation, eczema, hypertension, kidney trouble, eye infections, and several other diseases.

Avoid the table use of commercial "herb" salts, as garlic and celery salts, which unknown to the unsuspecting buyer contain a great deal of sodium chloride and very little herb. And in the preparation of pastries and cookies, try to do without bicarbonate of soda or baking soda.

To enjoy the true flavor of sodium and chlorine without harm and to one's benefit, partake of dark green lettuce, uncooked spinach, parsley, tomatoes, celery, carrots, and steamed kale, asparagus and turnips and all fresh fruits. The daily intake of these foods, as well as the frequent consumption of eggs, dairy products, sea foods and molasses, will more than adequately supply and satisfy one's salt requirement.

There are many people who heap the chemical salt on uncooked vegetables and fruits, on celery, apples, tomatoes, melon and grapefruit, in their soups and stews, and on meats and fish. In hot weather, the unwary are accustomed to use more and more of this dangerous chemical, for they are under the popular but mistaken impression that the body will suffer if the salt lost by perspiring is not quickly replaced. Dr. Herbert Shelton says, "that . . . gastric irritation due to the use of salt often gives rise to great and unquenchable thirst is well known. That the eating of heavily salted foods impairs digestion is, perhaps, not so well-known. Unsalted food is actually more easily digested than salted food." Benjamin Rush, surgeon-general of the Continental Army during the American Revolution, was told that the Indians used no salt in their foods. When Henry David Thoreau noted the same fact, he quickly abandoned the use of salt. The use of salted foods by sailors on the old sailing vessels may have been responsible for scurvy. By substituting fresh unsalted vegetables for salted foods, sailors would recover from scurvy. American sailors took along a supply of freshly collected herbs from which they prepared tisanes, drinking a cupful with each meal.

Here is my formula for Herb Salt.

Powder, mix well and sift: 3 parts basil, 2 savory, 2 celery seed, 2 sage, 1 thyme, 1 marjoram. Gain extra flavor by adding powdered sassafras or kelp (seaweed) or both.

Use your "herb salt" in soups, vegetable cocktails, meat and cheese sandwiches, cheese and sour-cream spreads, hors d'oeuvres, etc.

The following native herbs are easy to find and offer enough sodium and chlorine, in even small doses, to satisfy the daily requirement: sassafras leaves and bark, the leaves of wild carrot, nettles, maple, early tansy, peppergrass and trefoil, goldenrod, and the usually discarded leaves of beets, radishes, and garden carrots. Dried and powdered, they can be carefully sifted and mixed with your selection of aromatics. Other salt-substitute mixtures include: basil, marjoram, savory, dill, fennel, rosemary (sparingly), celery, thyme, and lovage leaf. A rule of thumb recipe I use is to mix equal portions of the non-aromatic natives, seasonings and of kelp.

One more nutritional caveat: it is the opinion of most nutritionists that white sugar is a deceptive food because it has been deprived of basic nutritional values and a dangerous food because it leaches out of the system the nutritive elements present there. Refined sugar robs the system of calcium vital to the teeth, bones, and blood, and contributes to tooth decay and organic disorders as nervousness and diabetes. It is important to remember that since much of the sugar is quickly absorbed in the intestinal tract, eating large quantities of it may overwhelm the liver's capacity to withdraw sugar from the blood and lead to hyperglycemia and the appearance of glucose in the urine, a condition known as alimentary glycosuria. It is therefore recommended that one who seeks better health should consume a minimum of such commercial "foods" as candy, canned foods, soft drinks, ice cream, cakes, custard, and especially soft drinks.

Use sources of natural sugars: honey—the "ambrosia of the gods," unsulfured molasses and raw brown sugar. Brown sugar, if raw and unprocessed, contains the vital nutritive values which the unhealthy white variety lacks. It, therefore, is recommended not only as food but as an ingredient in a variety of medicinal remedies. It can be used in the making of cough lozenges or drops and candied roots and leaves.

3

Growing Your Herb Garden

The least expensive and the most enjoyable way to provide your-self with culinary herbs is to grow them. An herb garden is a relatively simple endeavor and your only expense is that of a few packets of seeds. The requirements of soil conditions, sun, etc., apply equally to a two-by-four garden in a cramped back yard and a giant one in a twenty-acre estate.

Don't try to grow all the herbs discussed in this book during the first few years; do try five or six of the more hardy perennials, as lemon balm, sage and thyme, and have fun, both in the garden and kitchen. Experiment with easy varieties such as chives, basil and marjoram. Each year add one or two of your seed-bearing favorites, such as anise, caraway or fennel, and one or two herbs such as lavender and tarragon, which require special attention. Each year transplant the wild-growing angelica, wild ginger, tansy, various mints and wormwood into your garden.

The beginner would do well to start with a small plot—say, 4 by 16 feet, and allot an area of 2 feet to each herb. If you have a bit of extra space in your garden between your rows of vegetables, do consider growing such edible herbs as chives, chervil and parsley; they do well also as borders for separate beds or around the entire vegetable garden. However, such proximity to the vegetable garden is permissible only if this is your first venture in the culture of culinary herbs, because the effectiveness of herbs decreases with constant watering, such as a vegetable garden requires. Herbs also thrive in poor soil, contrary to vegetables. (But there is no hard rule for keeping separate the herbs from the vegetables. If necessary, grow the herbs wherever possible. Doing so may make the beginner more aware of still another of their helpful properties. One may employ a particular herb as a companion for that food which it is intended to season: savory for beans and peas, basil for tomatoes, etc.) Other cultivation sites include the back yard (but not near or with vegetables), along the border of the house, in a rock or roof garden and in boxes on the window sills of the kitchen and of other rooms.

Various herbs may be confined also to a narrow border of not more than 1½ feet, situated against the side of the garage and yard fence. One newspaper columnist offered this suggestion: "Rows of the flowering kinds of herbs can be planted in the most ordinary places to dress up drab sites on property." Keep chervil, chives and parsley in separate beds, near or outside the kitchen door. It is rewarding to have the herb garden at close hand, as Lucy H. Yates observed in 1842: "Take a little strip for the herbiary, let it be half way betwixt the flowers and vegetable garden, 'twill form a very appropriate transition stratum and may be the means of being more under the eye of the mistress, and thus of recovering to our soups and salads some of the comparatively neglected herbs of Tarragon and French Sorrel, of Purslane and Dill and Celery, and others whose place is nowhere to be found save in the pages of old herbalists."

To insure proper drainage the herb garden should if possible be located in an area that is slightly sloped. Most of the herbs grow well in dry soil, but during a long continued dry spell some watering would be required for the early seedlings.

Over-feeding or enriching of the soil is to be avoided, the better to insure the desired concentration of the aromatic principles of the herbs. They are not especially susceptible to plant diseases common to the ornamental flowers, and their aromatic foliage, in most cases, appears to be repellent to most insects.

Locate your herb garden where the sun's rays will produce their vitalizing warmth for at least 6–8 hours. The best position is south to southeast.

IN THE BACK YARD

A plot of ten-by-twenty feet is adequate. To avoid over-watering, the herbs should be cultivated in an area as remote as possible from the vegetable patch.

Have a separate bed for mints and one for other "spreaders" like thyme and chamomile. Label each section.

Keep the perennials together and a safe distance from the annual beds which must be dug up or turned over every fall.

IN A ROCK GARDEN

To those who complain that their yard is a monument to The Ice Age—with big rocks to the right, and giant rocks to the left—why not import a few more well-proportioned slabs of stone? Once added to the natural rocky design of the yard, these provide a pleasing base for a rock garden.

Fill in the stone spaces with alternate layers of well-decayed fall leaves, sand or small stones and peat moss.

Plant herbs of thyme, marjoram and pennyroyal, but do not crowd.

IN A WINDOW GARDEN, KITCHEN BOXES OR FLOWER POTS

Do you have a vacant window sill? Then utilize that area with a window-box or several flower pots of herbs. The window gardener who will set aside her sunny bay window for a set of herb boxes will be blessed with a crop of excellent food seasoners. (Window boxes are for either outdoors or indoors.) During the winter months, our window garden pays profitable dividends in sprouted onions and garlic whose greens grace our vegetable salad. To this are added pot-grown chives and parsley. Seeds collected in the fall and planted provide a constant supply of fresh greens, an economic and pleasing form of conservation. Winter culinaries include sage, thyme and lemon balm, and others later listed.

The window box should measure approximately 18 inches in length by 8 in depth, and 6 in width. Place a layer (about an inch) of broken stones spread at the bottom of the container, and two or three small holes cut for drainage. One can buy boxes that have false bottoms.

For all year round use, cultivate basil, chives, fennel, marjoram, the mints, fern-leafed parsley, and summer savory, to name only a few. Beware of a quick frost or the tender marjoram will be lost.

Do not crowd the plants.

Give the seedlings the needed sunny exposure.

Turn the boxes or pots around every few days to give each herb plant its share of sunshine.

Water the seedlings and young plants every day—but not too much, especially if they are in flower pots.

Cut the foliage down as needed for table use and to prevent the plants from assuming jungle proportions.

IN A ROOF GARDEN

Use wooden boxes either 12 inches long by 8 deep by 6 wide, or small barrel "thirds" (upper and lower sections that are tub shaped).

Choose the same herbs as for a window garden.

Transplant seedlings in late May, or early June.

AS A GROUND COVER

If your front lawn is one of those which has failed to respond to the effects of well-advertised fertilizers, you will find that thyme, chamomile, and mint are excellent ground covers, both novel and useful.

Plant your mint next to the house foundations; and thyme as a border edging.

Above all: *Do not add fertilizer of any kind to your soil.* Doing so invites disaster. Such enrichment will increase the size of the foliage and flowers but the quality of the fragrant oils, the essential property of herbs, will be greatly diminished, and the foliage less aromatic. However, in the fall a small amount of compost may be added to the soil where a perennial is being propagated by root division or layering.

A memory aid that might be helpful is: O-I-L is only three-quarters of S-O-I-L; thus Poor Soil = Oil = Taste = Culinary Success.

As important to the strength of the volatile oil is well-drained soil. Not even during drought do herblings such as marjoram and sage demand water, as do parsley and celery. The moisture extracted from the soil will suffice. But before planting do prepare the soil as indicated, or place a layer or two of small stones at the bottom of the bed. If you do not provide drainage your labor will prove fruitless.

Being resourceful organisms, herbs are, with few exceptions, not troubled by the proximity of weeds and grasses. Unless such wildings as purslane or lambsquarters actually begin to crowd out the young herb plants, there is no danger. I have always recommended to gardeners of herbs or of vegetables, that they first identify the economic use, if any, a wild-growing "weed" possesses before rooting up and discarding it as worthless. Chop up the discards and mix them into your compost mixture.

AN HERB WHEEL

If you would like to raise herbs, but your yard space is extremely limited, try an herb wheel. If your allotted area approximates roughly 4 by 4 feet and has full sun exposure, your herbs will thrive quite nicely in an old wagon wheel. As many as a dozen varieties can be grown between the wheel spokes.

To insure adequate sunlight for each plant, be sure to locate the smaller herbs in front of the taller ones.

If you answer "yes" to the following three questions, then you can be assured of a healthy crop of culinary herbs.

One: Have you poor garden soil?
Two: Is it well drained?
Three: Will you promise to pay less attention to your young herb plants than, say, to your vegetables?

Unless he is an organic gardener, the vegetable grower will apply expensive fertilizer to his farm or garden soil. Not so the herb-grower, for he seeks—if not cherishes—such soil usually considered valueless as far as vegetables are concerned. If the soil is loamy or garden rich, be sure to mix in thoroughly a 25–35% dilution of clean sand. In the springtime, roadside sand should be avoided. It often contains harmful salt that has been used to melt snow and ice. Lavender, for instance, will prove to be quite hardy if grown in sandy soil.

An herb garden is no different than the ordinary run of vegetable gardens, aside from water and soil requirements. I have recommended to beginners that in early February they and their friends, as one cooperative body, make arrangements with their local horticulturist so that anywhere from the last week of May up to the second or third week of June, he will have flats of young plants ready for transplanting into the garden.

The beginner is thus assured of healthy seedlings and a lower price per plant than bought individually. Bought separately, potted perennials average 50 cents apiece, and in a flat of 50 to 100, the average price is only six to fifteen cents each. For annuals, use the method of "direct sowing," described below.

Once you have collected your own basil or dill seeds and others you are assured of a good start the next season. There is a greater satisfaction to be received from such independence.

When planting in the seed bed make sure that the soil of seed flats contains $\frac{1}{3}$ sand, $\frac{2}{3}$ garden loam, sifted to eliminate stones.

When directly sowing annuals, prepare the soil, sow the seeds in late May and keep the rows at least a foot apart. Be careful to cover the seeds with only enough sifted soil to equal 2 to 3 times the diameter of the seeds. Shade with wetted cardboard or burlap and remove when germination begins. Don't let the soil dry out, but don't over-wet. When the seedlings have grown about five to six inches high, or when they have four true leaves, they must be thinned out to stand at least ten inches apart, or else later your plants will shade one another and the over-lapping of leaves will cause these plants to mold. The seedlings may also be placed in flower pots. Shade and water the young seedlings to help them recover from the shock of transplanting.

For anise, caraway, dill and other seed bearers, allow about nine to fifteen inches between seed rows. Anise and cumin must be sown in beds where they are to grow. The roots have such a frail network of fine threads that they do not recover easily from the shock of transplanting.

Consider fall sowing of herbs in the garden. With the sowing of fresh, ripened seed, one is assured of an early summer crop. In late October to early November, sow the seeds in shallow trenches and press down to insure their staying in place. When weather conditions are suitable and spring showers have done their job, the seedlings will appear. Several of the herbs suitable for fall planting are lemon balm, borage, burnet, caraway, chervil, dill, horehound, parsley, rue, summer savory and thyme.

The plant division system of propagation provides a continuous supply of herb plants for several years to come. The fourth year's growth of sage's root system, for instance, is very woody and the taste of the herb's leaves is disappointing. Plant division generally takes place on the plant's third birthday. With perennials, in general two-inch cuttings are taken in the spring and inserted into soil containing one-third sand or into vermiculite, and then thoroughly moistened. Water daily and protect with some shade. When these cuttings are well rooted, choose a cloudy day and transplant them to the more shaded part of your herb garden. If the cuttings are taken in the fall, store them in flower pots until needed for spring planting; but again be sure that the loam is not too rich. Mints are propagated by root cuttings.

In the case of chives, carefully separate the bulbs and carefully replant each. With chamomile, transplant a set of "runners" in gravelly sand and tread over by foot.

LAYERING   This is a method of propagating perennials like thyme, oregano and the mints. Cover carefully with soil the ends of the outer branches and water well every day. After a few weeks when they will have well rooted, cut the new plants from the parent. If they are to be transplanted, do so on a rainy or moist day.

Transplanting is the simple procedure of taking slips from the growing tips of the plants. Each slip should be no longer than three inches and show at least two nodes. Strip off most of the leaves and set the slip at right angles to root in sand or vermiculite. Water daily and protect from the sun. In three to five weeks the slips will have rooted well; either set them in pots or place them directly into the garden. Take cuttings of sage, rosemary, lemon balm and the mints.

ARRANGEMENT   Much too much, I sometimes think, has been written about the design of the herb garden. They are jig-saw puzzles at best, with their complicated, geometric designs which are called "knotted" gardens. A "knot" type of herb garden is patterned by the interesting paths and cross paths which divide the garden, for example, into quarters, resulting in four knots. Each quarter encloses a specific herb and is itself bordered by one or more edging plants.

Many of the contemporary herb "authorities" quote incessantly from the writings of Thomas Hyll, not to tell of the many economic uses of herbs but to delectate over wordy descriptions of the gardens that were fashionable in Queen Elizabeth's time. Rather than get yourself tangled up in knots, why not arrange your own garden pattern simply to contain a few crisscrossing squares and interlocking circles? Pick out your favorites according to size from the chart below and arrange first on paper a rough sketch of all the herbs concerned. "According to size" means assuring all herbs adequate benefits of the sun. Bear in mind the perennials must be kept together, away from the annuals and the biennials. The tall perennials, wormwood, catnip and tarragon, should be positioned in the rear of the garden; sage and savory to the center, and as borders marigold or anise are especially suitable.

Another type of bed may be made especially for the following perennials: thyme, lavender and rosemary, which enjoy living in a mixture of garden soil, old plaster rubble, charred wood and sand. Notice, especially, that each is of different height. Keep your mints in a more moist area.

Height of Full Grown Herbs

Annual	Inches	Biennial	Inches	Perennial	Inches
Anise	12–18	Angelica	60	Balm (lemon)	18–24
Basil (sweet)	10–24	Caraway	19–24	Burnet	24
Borage	18–24			Catnip	30–40
Chervil	10–15			Chives	9–12
Coriander	24			Fennel	48
Cumin	12			Hyssop	24–30
Dill	24–30			Marjoram	
Marigold	6–12			(sweet)	12–15
Summer				Oregano	24–36
savory	12			Oswego tea	18–30
				Parsley	9–12
				Peppermint	18–30
				Rosemary	12–24
				Rue	12–24
				Sage	18–24
				Savory	
				(winter)	16
				Tarragon	24–40
				Thyme	6–12
				Wormwood	30–36

COLLECTION AND PRESERVATION

To collect herbs, follow these rules carefully and your months of labors will be fruitful and will serve as an inducement to bigger and better herb gardens.

Most herbs are usually ready for cutting just before blossoming, especially thyme, summer savory, and marjoram. Lemon balm, basil, rosemary and sage will provide three or four cuttings during the outdoor growing season. Remember John Evelyn's advice regarding lavender, rosemary, sage, and thyme: "The more you clip them, the more they will thrive."

Gather the herbs on the second of two successive sunny days between 10 A.M. and noon. This will protect the plant from mold that results from the extra overdose of moisture. It is interesting to note that the later the hour on the day when the herb is collected, the poorer is the grade of the aromatic herb.

Cut only the upper half, thus providing for new growth. With sage, collect the upper third of the herb and lower leaves. Quick-growing borage may be collected every four to five weeks. Label each collection with name of herb and date of collection.

Seeds are collected just before "shattering" or as soon as they begin to ripen. The leaves of seed-bearing dill, anise and fennel may be collected for culinary use from late spring to fall. To save all seeds it is best to cover these herbs with cheesecloth after they have been cut and allowed to dry.

To dry, tie small bundles of the herb with string and suspend them as near to the ceiling as possible, and preferably in a warm attic or in the shade of the rear hallway near the kitchen where there is good circulation of air. Aromatic herbs dry best at an average temperature of 70°. For seeds and roots, I recommend a 2–3 foot wooden rack of cheesecloth or fine mesh wire. To hasten drying, stir or mix the seeds or roots every day or so.

Above all, do not crowd the herbs or permit them to overlap, for this causes drying herbs to mold or blacken, and all your efforts will have been wasted.

Do not dry your aromatic herbs with heat.

To preserve, when thoroughly dry, the leaves should be ground up as finely as needed and the coarse stems removed. Preserve in absolutely dry Mason or suitable air-tight glass jars, previously washed and cleaned with hot water and soap. Label each jar with the name of the herb, its variety or Latin name, location and date of collection.

The dating of the collection is important since the aromatic herbs and spices do lose their flavor with age. Herbs should not be used for seasonings two years after their collection but may be consigned to the vinegar jar.

Store all herbs in a cool place.

Enjoy them throughout the fall, winter and spring.

4

Using Culinaries

There are no hard and fast rules that apply to the use of herbs as seasonings. You must learn by trial and error just which and how much of each herb will suit your particular taste. Remember it is better to use too little than too much. I recommend the "French method": A little bit of this, a little bit of that, and a pinch of this and that. Add the herbs with a teasing touch. " 'Tis wiser to taunt than to tire the taste, and a nice moderation guards against waste." Accentuate a dish by slow addition and you won't be sorry. Study the personality and flavor of each herb and of various herb blends, just as the artist studies his pigments and their blends.

Here are some general principles I find useful to keep in mind when I am seasoning with herbs. Experiment with different combinations of herbs and let each combination be so subtle that no one herb predominates.

Do season sparingly until you are well acquainted with the aromatic strength of each herb:

A "pinch" of a dried herb is enough to season two to three food portions.

Always add your herbs towards the end of the cooking period, unless otherwise directed. The delicate flavor and aroma of our savory herbs are lost when they are submitted to prolonged heat.

Do not flavor more than one dish of the same meal with the same herb. Do not use too many herbs at one meal.

Resist the temptation of using herbs with every dish—morning, noon, and night.

Taste the makings as you go along.

Consult the charts often. Vary the same recipes with different herbs. You may use any herb in combination with one or more as shown in the charts. In time you will replace old cooking habits with daring and imaginative creations of your own.

Acquaint yourself with herb taste-values by drinking freshly prepared teas of your favorite herbs.

Remember that variations in the taste of the same kinds of food is nil; only the seasoning is different.

Bring out the aromatic oils of the fresh herbs, their leaves or seeds, by crushing or chopping them before using. Dried herbs may be previously soaked in oil or wine or vinegar.

Complex recipes have their place in cooking but often diminish the nutrients in food and destroy its natural taste. Culinary herbs will help you to stay closer to naturally delicious and healthful foods and away from canned processed products.

Which of all the dozens of culinary herbs should be considered best and given top priority for seasoning one's foods? Such a list is a matter of individual opinion, more perhaps the result of one's experiences in the art of seasoning. It is the contention of many herbalists and chefs that in the beginning, the neophyte acquire and use not more than 10 or 12 herbs. This number is sufficient to season almost every food and prepare a complete variety of dressings, sauces and jellies. (Of more than 300 native herbs, I consider only 25 as useful for my everyday needs).

Highly recommended culinaries are basil, fennel, marjoram, mints, oregano, rosemary, sage, summer savory and thyme. Later, as one gains experience in herb cookery, caraway, dill, and tarragon may be added to the list.

Remember that although parsley, chives and celery are often recommended as seasoning herbs, they are foods that must be eaten in their uncooked state if one is to benefit from their high-potency blood-fortifying nutrients.

Here are basic combinations for meat and fish:

MEAT BLEND			
Marjoram	3	parts	(or teaspoonfuls)
Rosemary	2	parts	
Savory	2	parts	
Thyme	1	part	
Sage	1	part	

These are dried herbs. Mix and use one teaspoonful for each pound of meat.

FISH BLEND		
Basil	½	part
Balm	½	part
Oregano	½	part
Dill	1	part
Thyme	1	part
Savory	2	parts

These are dried herbs. Mix and use one teaspoonful for each pound of fish or pint of fish chowder.

My four basic herb seasonings are basil, marjoram, summer savory and thyme. Build your flavor combinations around these. Add or subtract as you wish. Instead of basil, you may prefer oregano, or sage.

The term kitchen bouquet or *bouquet garni* applies to a mixture of dried herbs, i.e. freshly dried, contained in a cheesecloth bag. Tie a string or thread to it for easy removal. The bag is placed directly into the soup or stew, there to remain for the desired length of seasoning time. The bag is removed before serving. The herbs are basil, marjoram, rosemary, summer savory, thyme and sage.

The term *aux fines herbes* refers to a mixture of finely ground fresh or dried herbs, that is mixed with, or sprinkled over the dish in preparation (eggs, cheese, fish, and meat dishes) and eaten with the food. Herbs added to the butter before an omelette is prepared will impart more lasting flavor than if they are merely sprinkled over the eggs. *Aux fines herbes* are basil, celery seed, chervil, chives, marjoram, mint, sweet savory, parsley, sage, tarragon and thyme. If chervil, chives and parsley are included in a recipe, they should be freshly cut and added to the food after it is cooked. The mixture of other herbs is added to the food during the last few minutes of cooking. Prepare several blends of dried herbs, label each container and store for future use. *Aux fines herbes* help to add flavor to roasts and chopped meats and go well with broiled fish. They are also delicious in egg omelettes and salads.

For fruit and vegetable salads, steep the herbs in hot water for 5 to 8 minutes before using. This will bring out the flavor. Then mix in the herbs with the other ingredients.

Vegetable salad herbs include celery leaves, chives, fennel, parsley, burnet, dill, basil, chervil, watercress, tarragon and chicory.

Soup, stews and gravy will be enhanced by immersing an herb bouquet in the liquid a few minutes before it is finished, but only long enough to bring out the desired flavor. If the herbs are left too long, they may impart an unpleasant taste. A bouquet for soup is quickly composed by mixing together one teaspoonful each of thyme, basil, marjoram, and one-half teaspoonful of savory and one-quarter sage. (Add ground lemon, orange, or tangerine peels, if desired.) The bouquet bag is suspended in or added to the soup or stew near the end of the cooking process, remaining there 15–25 minutes. Modify the process according to the desired strength of herb flavor.

A SAMPLING OF HERB RECIPES

Sauces and Dressings

HERB SAUCE
BASIC RECIPE

1 cup milk
½–1 tsp. butter
2 Tb. flour
⅛–½ tsp. powdered kelp
A tiny dash paprika or curry (optional)
1 heaping tsp. herbs

To thin, decrease butter and flour. To thicken, increase the butter and flour.

Instead of milk you may substitute ⅔ cup of white wine and a tablespoonful of herb vinegar.

Herbs: basil, celery seed, garlic or onion powder, oregano, sage, tarragon and thyme. The herbs should be very finely ground or powdered.

The sauce may be quickly prepared by stirring well a sufficient quantity of the powdered herb or herbs to a measure of lemon juice and melted butter. However, it is best to have the herbs stay moistened in the liquid for 20–30 minutes before incorporating.

Don't forget to put extra flavor in your tartar or hollandaise sauce with finely ground tarragon, one-quarter teaspoonful to a cupful of prepared sauce.

FISH SAUCE

2 Tb. butter or margarine
2 Tb. flour
1 cup milk
1½ tsp. thyme
¼–½ tsp. basil
½ tsp. vegetized salt or kelp
Dash of paprika

Melt the butter or margarine in the flour and add the milk gradually. Mix and add the other ingredients. Serve the sauce over the fish or on the side.

TOMATO HERB
SAUCE I

Cup of fresh tomatoes
½ cup water
½ tsp. garlic powder
2 Tb. butter (or margarine)
Dash paprika
Slice of lemon
½ tsp. thyme

Simmer all ingredients except thyme and butter (or margarine) until tomatoes are very soft.

Rub through a strainer. Then add butter and thyme.

TOMATO HERB
SAUCE II

2 cups (2 8 oz. cans) tomato sauce
1 Tb. minced onion
1 tsp. crumbled whole oregano leaves
1 tsp. crumbled basil leaves
Minced onion for garnish (optional)
   Cook all ingredients together in a saucepan for
10 minutes. If desired, garnish with minced onion.

DUCK SAUCE

Beat into a glassful of currant jelly a tablespoonful each of mint leaves and grated orange
rinds. Let stand 2 hours before serving.

VEGETABLE
SAUCE I

Beat 2 egg yolks into ¾ cup of sour cream, and
incorporate ¼ teaspoonful summer savory and 2
teaspoonsful of tarragon vinegar or other herb
vinegar. Place the mixture in double boiler and
cook, stirring constantly until thickened. Serve
over steamed vegetables such as broccoli or cauliflower.

VEGETABLE
SAUCE II

1 Tb. butter
2 tsp. lemon juice
1 Tb. chopped chives
2 Tb. flour
¼ tsp. mixed herbs; basil, oregano or marjoram
   Simmer the chives in the butter for a few minutes. Add the flour, stir smooth, and cook for 3
minutes. Add the herbs, cook until thickened
and smooth, and lastly add the lemon juice. Stir
well and remove.

SAUCE PIQUANTE

1. Place a Tb. of butter in a pan and add 2
sliced onions. Saute until onions are soft.
   2. Add two carrots and two parsnips, thyme,
basil, 2 cloves, 2 shallots (or leeks) and one clove
of garlic.
   3. Stir until well-colored.
   4. Add flour and moisten with some broth and
½ tablespoonful each of wine and of vinegar.
   5. Skim, strain and add a dash of kelp.

ITALIAN SAUCE

1. Put a Tb. of butter into the pan, melt and
add sliced mushrooms and onions, parsley and a
crumbled bay leaf.

2. Stir the ingredients several times, and shake in a little flour; moisten with equal parts wine and broth, adding salt substitute and a pinch of mace. Mix well.

3. Heat for half hour; then skim away fat. Add a *bouquet garni* of basil and oregano, and remove before serving.

CLARET HERB SAUCE

½ cup claret
1 cup brown sugar
½ cup water
¼ tsp. each of 3 herbs: rosemary, thyme, oregano, marjoram or basil

Simmer the herbs in water in a covered pan for 20–30 minutes, allow to cool and strain. Prepare a syrup of the sugar and water and mix with the wine.

Note: Honey may be substituted for the syrup.

Try other dry or semi-dry wines, such as burgundy or sauterne, with these herbs.

TARTAR SAUCE

1 cup mayonnaise
2 Tb. chopped cucumbers and chives
1 Tb. chopped parsley
Season to taste (with ground herbs)

Mix well and serve.

HERBED HOLLANDAISE SAUCE

½ cup butter
Juice of ½ lemon
2 egg yolks
½ cup boiling water
Choice of herbs

Beat together the butter, egg yolks and lemon juice. Heat in double-boiler until the sauce begins to thicken. Then add the boiling water, beating all the time. Remove from the water as soon as it is the consistency of soft custard. Do not overcook.

HONEY-MINT SAUCE

½ cup meat stock or vegetable juice
1 Tb. cider vinegar
1 cup honey
¼ cup chopped mint

Heat together stock and vinegar. Add the honey and stir well. Add mint. Simmer for 5 minutes. This sauce can be used to baste chops or lamb roasts, or served with lamb at the table. Yields 1½ cups.

SOUR CREAM FISH SAUCE

1½ cups sour cream
1½ Tb. herb vinegar
⅛ tsp. basil, oregano or thyme
1 egg
1 tsp. cornstarch
⅛ tsp. powdered garlic or onion
¼ tsp. powdered mustard
Add kelp to taste
Beat the ingredients together and cook in top section of double-boiler over gently boiling water. Stir about 5–7 minutes until thickened.

BASIC TOMATO SAUCE

Cook together for 15 minutes:
½ can tomatoes
1 slice onion
1 bay leaf
1 Tb. chopped green pepper
½ tsp. salt substitute
1 tsp. brown sugar
Strain. Thicken by stirring in 1 Tb. butter and 2 Tb. flour blended together; add 1 tsp. chopped parsley and a pinch of savory. For Spanish sauce to serve with an omelette, add 2 or 3 cut-up olives and a dash of paprika.

SPAGHETTI SAUCE

Sage and rosemary are a delightful combination of flavors in a rich-red tomato sauce for spaghetti. Add to the above recipe. Add mushrooms if you like. The herbs give the dish an appetite-teasing aroma that will have your family lining up hungrily long before the dinner-bell rings!

SPAGHETTI WITH GREEN SAUCE

Brown 2 cloves minced garlic in ⅓ cup each of olive oil and butter. Add 2 Tb. each chopped parsley, chives, pine nuts (optional), 1½ Tb. dried mint leaves, ½ tsp. salt substitute, ¼ tsp. each black pepper (optional), basil. Cook 1–2 minutes.

Mix with 1 pound cooked spaghetti and ¼ cup grated Parmesan cheese.

HERBED
MAYONNAISE

Perk up your mayonnaise with the addition of small amounts of finely chopped fresh herbs plus chives, chervil and parsley. Add a little vinegar.

BASIC SALAD
DRESSING

7 oz. vegetable oil
1 oz. cider or herb vinegar
1 clove garlic, finely cut
¼ tsp. each basil and oregano
(The garlic and vinegar may be replaced with 1 oz. of garlic vinegar.)

HERB SALAD
DRESSING

⅛ cup tarragon vinegar (or your favorite herb vinegar)
⅛ tsp. kelp (optional)
⅛ tsp. raw brown sugar
1 small clove garlic
1 cup soy bean or peanut oil
1 tsp. lemon juice (or finely cut peel)
½ oz. dry wine
Herbs: basil, oregano, sage, thyme and summer savory
   Directions: Use about a tsp. of the mixed, ground herbs. Steep them overnight in a mixture of the wine and vinegar. Crush the garlic and mix the juice with the kelp and wine-vinegar mixture, and to this add the oil, and beat well. This preparation may be refrigerated. Shake well before serving.
   Salad dressing tastes better with either fresh (finely ground and sifted) burnet or chervil, a teaspoonful to a cup of dressing. Add the herbs just before serving.

SOUR CREAM
FOR CUCUMBERS

1 cup sour cream
¾ tsp. kelp
1 Tb. brown raw sugar
2 Tb. tarragon or other herb vinegar
2 Tb. chopped chives
1 tsp. each dill and celery seed
   Mix and pour dressing over cucumbers which

have been sliced and chilled for an hour or two and drained. Sprinkle with paprika.

CELERY SEED
DRESSING

Mix together 2 ounces (4 Tb.) each of salad oil, honey and lemon juice. To this, add slowly ½ to ¾ tsp. of celery seed. Mix thoroughly.

HERB FRENCH
DRESSING I

1 cup salad oil
⅓ cup tarragon vinegar
1 bruised clove garlic
1 tsp. chives or grated onion
1 tsp. brown sugar
Paprika
1 tsp. dried mixed herbs or
1 tsp. each of fresh basil, tarragon, chervil and parsley
Shake thoroughly in a jar. Let stand several hours or overnight, then strain and store.

HERB FRENCH
DRESSING II

3 Tb. salad oil
1 Tb. lemon juice or vinegar
1 generous pinch paprika
¼ tsp. chopped chives
⅛ tsp. chopped thyme
⅛ tsp. chopped sweet marjoram
Bruise the herbs well and mix all the ingredients together. Shake well in a bottle before using. (Keep in refrigerator for future use.)

BASIC FRENCH
DRESSING

¼ cup cider vinegar
(or mint, tarragon, dill vinegar, etc.)
2 Tbs. honey
⅓ cup oil
⅛ tsp. salt (optional)

TOMATO JUICE
DRESSING

¼ cup tomato juice
¼ cup cider (or herb) vinegar
2 Tb. honey
2 Tb. nutritional yeast
1 egg yolk
2 Tb. chives
1 sprig parsley
½ cup oil
Blend all ingredients, except oil, until well

blended. Gradually add oil. Blend until smooth. Makes one cup.

CHEDDAR CHEESE
DRESSING

1 cup yoghurt (or sour cream)
1 cup cheddar cheese grated
¼ cup cider (or herb) vinegar
1 tsp. caraway seeds
  Blend all ingredients. Makes 2½ cups.

CUCUMBER
DRESSING

1 cup cucumber, diced
1 cup yoghurt
1 Tb. cider (or herb) vinegar
Pinch of salt substitute
1 sprig dill
½ tsp. dill seeds
  Blend all ingredients. Makes 2 cups.

SOUR CREAM
DRESSING

1 cup sour cream
2 Tb. herb vinegar
1 Tb. honey
  Blend well and serve.

SWEET CREAM
SALAD DRESSING

1 egg
Juice of 1 lemon
1 cup sweet cream
  Beat the egg well, stir in the sweet cream and add the lemon juice.

EGG DRESSING

2 eggs
½ cup salad oil
Juice of ½ lemon
¼ tsp. finely ground herbs (your choice)
  Beat the eggs and oil together and add the lemon juice and herbs.

Herb Spreads

HERBED CREAM
CHEESE

Moisten 1 large cake Philadelphia cream cheese with cream until it will spread easily. Add salt substitute, 1 Tb. each of minced parsley and chopped chives; ½ tsp. of minced garlic or onion greens. Add dill, marjoram and rosemary to taste. It is better to make it up 24 hours ahead. Check the seasoning before using. Spread on very thinly sliced bread, garnish with a sprig of parsley or chervil.

SOUR CREAM AND
HERB MIX FOR
HORS D'OEUVRES

1 cup sour cream
1 tsp. finely chopped chives
1 tsp. finely chopped rosemary
1 tsp. finely chopped thyme
1 tsp. finely chopped parsley
1 tsp. finely chopped dill
1 tsp. finely choped tarragon
1 tsp. finely chopped sage
1 tsp. finely chopped basil
½ tsp. finely chopped lovage
    Mix well

HERBED COTTAGE
CHEESE I

2 pint (16 oz.) containers cottage cheese
2 small packages cream cheese
½ cup mixed herbs cut very fine—chives, chervil, marjoram, thyme, parsley, savory, mint, sorrel, tarragon
¼ cup oil and herb vinegar
    Soak the herbs in the dressing for an hour. Blend the 2 cheeses together and season with salt substitute, a pinch of powdered celery seed, minced onion, and paprika. Blend in the soaked herbs and sprinkle with paprika. Tastes better if it stands 24 hours. Will keep several days in the refrigerator. Serve spread on crackers or whole wheat bread. Do not spread too far ahead or bread or crackers will become soggy.

HERBED COTTAGE
CHEESE II

    Another favorite recipe is cottage cheese mixed with chopped chives, thyme and sweet marjoram. With this mixture remember to bruise the herbs well before adding. Add a salt substitute to taste. A little cream may be stirred in. It adds a great deal to the richness and flavor. Then add:
1 tsp. chopped chives
⅛ tsp. chopped thyme
⅛ tsp. chopped sweet marjoram
    Bruise the herbs well and let stand a half hour before serving.

SOY SPREAD
½ cup soy flour (or whole wheat flour)
½ cup peanut butter
1 Tb. nutritional yeast
3 Tb. chives chopped
3 Tb. parsley
½ cup favorite dressing
(Add also ½ tsp. ground dill seed.)
   Blend all ingredients together until smooth. Makes about 1½ cups.

COTTAGE CHEESE
SPREAD
½ lb. cottage cheese
¼ tsp. each of celery, dill and caraway seeds
⅛ tsp. salt substitute
3 Tb. nutritional yeast
1 Tb. parsley minced
1 Tb. onion grated
3 Tb. soy flour
¼ cup wheat germ

SOUR CREAM
SPREAD
¾ cup sour cream
2 Tb. tarragon vinegar
4 scallions finely chopped
3 Tb. parsley, cut fine
2 Tb. olive oil (or other vegetable oil)
A dash of paprika
   Blend the oil slowly into the sour cream, stir in the vinegar, add the other ingredients. Add enough paprika to color.

Herb Butters

TARRAGON
BUTTER
½ cup butter (softened)
1 sprig fresh tarragon minced
1 tsp. nutritional yeast
1 tsp. lemon juice
1 Tb. parsley
   Blend all ingredients. Use over broiled fish, broccoli and asparagus.

DILL BUTTER
½ cup butter
1 sprig fresh dill minced
½ tsp. dill seeds crushed
1 tsp. nutritional yeast

1 tsp. lemon juice
1 Tb. parsley, minced
    Blend ingredients. Use with fish or baked potato. Makes about ¾ cup.

LEMON HERB
BUTTER

½ cup butter softened
1 Tb. lemon rind grated
½ tsp. basil minced
½ tsp. chervil minced
1 Tb. parsley minced
1 Tb. chives minced
    Blend ingredients. Use with fish or vegetables. Makes about ¾ cup.

HERB BUTTER

¼ lb. butter
2 tsp. finely chopped parsley
2 tsp. finely chopped chives
½ tsp. lemon juice
1 small clove garlic (pressed)
2 tsp. finely chopped tarragon
    Add herbs and juice to softened butter and cream all together. Cover and store in refrigerator for all flavors to macerate.

Grains and Vegetables

BUCKWHEAT
GROATS (Kasha)

    In a saucepan saute an onion in oil until brown. Beat an egg in a dish and add a cup of groats. Add 2 cups of water to the sauted onion and stir in the groat mixture, 1 tsp. caraway seeds and 2 Tb. sesame seeds. Cover tightly and bring to a boil. Cook over low heat until buckwheat is tender.

BARLEY-LENTIL
KASHA

½ cup whole barley
1 cup lentils, soaked
¼ cup soy grits
Hot seasoned stock to cover
3 Tb. nutritional yeast
1 onion sliced and sauted
3 Tb. parsley minced
1 tsp. rosemary
    Combine barley, lentils and soy grits in sauce-

pan. Add with stock to depth of ½ inch above mixture. Cover and simmer gently until barley and lentils are tender. Add rest of ingredients and if necessary, more stock. Simmer 10 minutes longer. Serves 6.

BAKED POTATOES
WITH HERBS

Bake 4 large potatoes until they are soft when squeezed. Cut in half along lengthwise and scoop out the inside. Mash this and mix with 3 Tb. butter and enough heavy cream to make a fluffy consistency. Add ½ tsp. minced thyme, ½ tsp. chervil, ½ tsp. chopped chives, and a tiny bit of sage. Mix well, refill potato skins loosely. Reheat in a slow oven.

HERB STEAMED
RICE

1 cup brown, raw rice
2 cups seasoned stock (vegetable)
2 Tb. oil
3 Tb. nutritional yeast
3 Tb. parsley, minced
1 tsp. marjoram
   Heat stock in top of double boiler over direct heat. When boiling, add rice, oil and yeast. Place over bottom of double boiler to which hot water has been added. Cook gently for 30 to 40 minutes or until grains have absorbed all liquid. Garnish with parsley and marjoram. Serves 6.

HERBED ZUCCHINI

4 small zucchini sliced
1 Tb. butter
2 Tb. oil
1 clove garlic
1 small onion
½ bay leaf
1 tsp. minced basil
⅓ cup consomme or vegetable broth
2 fresh peeled tomatoes or same amount canned tomatoes
   Cook onion and garlic in butter and oil without browning. Add zucchini, herbs and consomme. Cover and cook 10 minutes. Add to-

matoes and finish cooking. Add 1 Tb. Parmesan
cheese (optional) before serving.

TOMATO JUICE
COCKTAIL

From 6 to 24 hours before you plan to serve, add
to 1 pint tomato juice: ½ tsp. each minced basil,
thyme, marjoram, summer savory and tarragon;
1 tsp. chopped chives. Steep and just before serving add juice of 1 lemon. Strain and serve chilled.

HERBED
MUSHROOM
CASSEROLE

4 cups mushrooms, sliced
¼ cup oil
1 tsp. marjoram
½ tsp. rosemary
3 Tb. nutritional yeast
½ cup seasoned stock (vegetable juice)
  Saute mushrooms briefly in oil. Add remaining
ingredients. Turn into casserole. Bake at 350°
for 20 minutes. Serves 6.

MUSHROOMS
POLONAISE WITH
DILL

1 lb. fresh mushrooms
1 clove garlic
1 tsp. sea salt
¼ tsp. pepper
6 Tb. butter
Few sprigs fresh dill, or tsp. dried dill
1½ cups sour cream
Chopped parsley
  Wipe mushrooms clean (do not wash) and slice.
Add all the herbs and seasonings to the sour
cream. Melt butter, add mushrooms and saute 2
to 3 minutes. Add sour cream mixture and allow
to simmer gently for 5 minutes. Do *not* boil.
Serve on buttered toast points or rusks.

TOMATO SALAD
WITH OREGANO

2 fresh tomatoes
⅛ tsp. garlic powder
1 tsp. crumbled whole oregano leaves
2 Tb. olive or salad oil
2 Tb. wine vinegar
  Wash tomatoes and cut each into 4 crosswise
slices. Combine remaining ingredients and sprinkle over tomatoes. Serve alone as a vegetable or

as salad on lettuce with slices of red, sweet Spanish onions. Serves 4.

HERBED
WHOLEWHEAT
STRAWS

2⅔ cup wholewheat flour
⅔ cup oil
1 cup cold water or potato water
3 Tb. mixed herbs (rosemary, basil, marjoram, oregano, etc.)

Blend all ingredients, adding enough liquid to make stiff dough. Chill. Roll out on floured pastry board—cut into strips 1 × 3 inches. Bake at 400° for about 10 minutes. Makes 4–5 dozen straws.

SAVORY NUT LOAF

1 cup ground cereals or bread crumbs
3 cups finely chopped vegetables
2 cups thin nut butter dressing
1 Tb. savory herbs (marjoram, sage, or savory)
1 Tb. chopped parsley

Mix well, put into an oiled pan and bake in a moderately hot oven for about 45 minutes.

Affinities Between Herbs and Vegetables

Artichoke	Oregano, Thyme
Asparagus	Caraway, Rosemary, Tarragon, Thyme
Beans, Baked, Lima	Marjoram, Sage, Summer Savory, Tarragon, Thyme
Beans, String	Basil, Caraway, Dill, Oregano, Rosemary, Sage, Summer Savory
Beet	Caraway, Dill, Fennel, Marjoram, Summer Savory, Thyme
Broccoli	Basil, Chamomile, Dill, Oregano
Brussels Sprouts	Basil, Caraway, Dill, Sage
Cabbage*	Basil, Caraway, Dill, Marjoram, Mint, Oregano, Summer Savory
Carrot*	Basil, Caraway, Mint, Sage, Thyme
Cauliflower*	Caraway, Cumin, Dill, Oregano, Rosemary, Summer Savory, Tarragon
Cucumber*	Basil, Dill
Eggplant	Basil, Marjoram, Rosemary, Sage, Thyme
Lentil	Oregano, Summer Savory
Mushroom	Tarragon, Thyme
Onion*	Basil, Caraway, Coriander, Oregano, Rosemary, Sage, Thyme

Pea	Basil, Marjoram, Mint, Oregano, Rosemary, Summer Savory
Pepper, Green*	Marjoram, Thyme
Potato	Caraway, Mint, Oregano, Rosemary, Thyme
Rice	Basil, Saffron, Marigold, Marjoram, Oregano, Summer Savory
Sauerkraut	Caraway, Fennel, Marjoram
Spinach*	Marjoram, Oregano, Rosemary
Squash, Summer	Basil, Dill, Marjoram, Rosemary, Sage, Savory
Squash, Winter	Caraway, Dill
Tomato*	Basil, Dill, Oregano, Sage, Summer Savory, Tarragon
Turnip	Caraway, Dill, Rosemary, Summer Savory
Watercress*	Thyme

* Best eaten uncooked.

Meat and Poultry Affinities

Beef	Basil, Fennel, Marjoram, Sage, Savory, Thyme
Chicken	Marjoram, Oregano, Saffron, Sage, Summer Savory, Tarragon, Thyme
Duck	Rosemary, Sage, Tarragon, Thyme
Lamb	Basil, Dill, Marjoram, Mint, Rosemary, Summer Savory, Thyme
Liver	Basil, Cumin, Summer Savory
Pork	Basil, Marjoram, Oregano, Rosemary, Sage, Lemon peel, Summer Savory, Thyme
Sausage	Basil, Marjoram, Oregano, Sage
Tongue	Marjoram, Thyme
Turkey	Rosemary, Tarragon, Thyme
Veal	Basil, Marjoram, Oregano, Rosemary, Summer Savory, Tarragon, Thyme
Venison	Basil, Marjoram, Oregano, Rosemary, Thyme

Note: For each 1½ pounds of hamburger, use a half teaspoonful each of marjoram and summer savory. Use only one or two herbs for each food, not a combination of herbs.

CHESTNUT DRESSING (for 9–10 lb. turkey)	2 cups chestnut meats (Roast chestnuts 15–20 minutes in 350° oven. Shell when warm.)
	3 cups stale bread crumbs
	1 large onion minced

2 large stalks celery minced
2 Tb. minced parsley
1 Tb. minced fresh sage
1 Tb. minced fresh sweet marjoram
1½ tsp. kelp
1 tsp. freshly ground pepper
1 beaten egg
Warm water or wine to moisten

Use fresh herbs when possible. If dry, use less and let stand in water or wine for a while to blend.

BRAISED TONGUE

1 fresh beef tongue
⅓ cup diced carrots
⅓ cup diced onions
⅓ cup diced celery
½ cup red wine
1 sprig parsley
1 sprig thyme
1 sprig marjoram
1 bay leaf

Wipe tongue and put in kettle. Cover with boiling water, and let simmer 2 hours. Take tongue from water, remove skin and roots. Place in deep baking pan and surround with vegetables and herbs. Pour over 4 cups of the stock and wine. Cover closely and bake 2 hours, turning after the first hour.

ORANGE BAKED
CHICKEN

1 frying chicken (2½ to 3 lbs.) cut in quarters
½ clove garlic
½ tsp. paprika
½ cup orange juice
1 Tb. grated orange rind
¼ tsp. ground rosemary (or ½ tsp. fresh leaf)
Pinch black pepper
1 small onion sliced thin

Rub chicken pieces with garlic clove. Arrange in baking dish. Sprinkle pieces with paprika, rosemary and pepper. Pour orange juice over and around chicken. Arrange onion slices over chicken. Cover and bake 45 minutes in moderately slow oven (350°). Remove cover and bake ½ hour longer or till fork tender and golden brown. Baste frequently with juice. Serves four.

LAMB BASTING LIQUID (for 4–6 pound roast)

Mix a half cup of bouillon or consomme, a half cup of white wine, one clove of garlic, minced, 2 Tb. of minced fresh (or a half Tb. of dried) mint, a half an onion, minced, and ¼ tsp. of marjoram or oregano. For variety, the mint may be replaced with a half tsp. of dried rosemary. The basting liquid is simmered for 5 minutes before the basting begins. Baste the roast with the liquid every 15 minutes, dipping it up from the roaster when you've used up the original mixture.

SAGE STUFFING (for small turkey)

1 medium onion, finely chopped
1 Tb. margarine
2 tsp. finely ground sage
1 tsp. powdered sea weed (kelp)
¼ tsp. pepper
⅔ cup melted margarine
⅓ cup boiling water
4 cups stale bread, cut in small cubes

Fry onion slowly in 1 Tb. margarine till clear and tender. Combine seasonings, melted butter, water and onions. Place bread in large bowl. Add butter mixture gradually, tossing lightly with fork as you add. Stir until well blended. Makes a fairly dry dressing that is enough for a 4–6 lb. turkey. If a more moist dressing is desired, add another ¼ cup water. One tsp. of marjoram or summer savory (or ½ tsp. of each) may be added to counterbalance the sage.

SAVORY POULTRY STUFFING

2 cups whole wheat bread crumbs
2 Tb. onion or garlic
    Raisins or currants
    Margarine or chicken fat
    Chestnuts, peanuts, pecans, vegetable leftovers, celery or parsley, diced apple, rinds of orange, lemon, tangerine and grapefruit
Herbs: basil, marjoram, oregano, rosemary, sage, summer savory, thyme. Use ½ tsp. of any 4 or 5 of your choice.
Optional: ½ cup of dry white wine.
NOTE: Use one tsp. of dried herbs (or one Tb. of fresh herbs) to each cup of bread crumbs.

HERB STUFFING
(turkey)

2 tsp. dried sage

1 tsp. dried savory

2 tsp. dried parsley

1 tsp. dried thyme

Salt, pepper and onion
to taste

1 egg beaten

15 slices toast

Pour warm water over toast—break slices with fork—add all other ingredients and mix thoroughly. I add prunes to this as my family enjoy them. Use ½ recipe for a large chicken.

THE ALL-AMERI-
CAN "HERB-
BURGERS"

Proper seasoning can make your hamburgers distinctive. Before broiling one pound of hamburger meat, add ¼ tsp. of garlic powder, 1 tsp. of dried parsley flakes, ⅛ tsp. of thyme and ⅛ tsp. of sage.

CHICKEN WITH
HERBS

Slice 2 cups of cold chicken. Add 1 cup chicken broth. Season with ½ tsp. each of burnet, chives, rosemary, tarragon, thyme, all finely chopped, and a pinch of dried celery leaves. Let it stand in double boiler (without boiling) to blend flavors, and serve hot.

MINCED LAMB

2 cups cold roast lamb, ground

Crumbs of two slices of white bread

2 eggs lightly beaten

½ cup lamb gravy

1 tsp. dried celery leaves

⅛ tsp. nutmeg

½ tsp. summer savory

Put in greased baking dish in pan of water; cover and bake for ½ hour in 375° oven. Uncover and brown for ½ hour more.

CHICKEN AND
RICE SUSSEX

Into buttered baking dish put:

1 cup diced cooked chicken

¾ cup uncooked rice

1 cup fresh mushrooms sauted

Blanched almonds (about 15 or so)

¼ tsp. finely chopped thyme

¼ tsp. finely chopped rosemary

½ tsp. salt substitute

Over this pour 2½ cups liquid (broth from chicken) and bake without any stirring until rice is flaky and tender and top is delicate brown (about 50 minutes at 350°).

Fish

FILLET OF FISH
BAKED WITH
HERBED BREAD
CRUMBS

1½ lbs. fillet of haddock, halibut or other fish
6 slices butter or margarine
3 cups soft bread crumbs
¾ to 1 tsp. vegetized salt or kelp
¼ tsp. crumbled whole oregano leaves
¼ tsp. crumbled whole marjoram leaves

Cut fish into 6 serving pieces. Place in a buttered 9-inch baking pan. Over each serving, sprinkle a dash of salt and place a slice of butter or margarine. Combine remaining ingredients, cover each serving with ½ cup of the mixture. Bake 25 to 30 minutes or until crumbs are brown in a preheated moderate oven (350°). Serves six.

COD FILLETS

Take fillets of fresh codfish; if there is skin, scald a few minutes and remove it, retaining the liquor. Lay fish in a buttered baking dish and prepare the following:
Cook 2 tomatoes with a small onion minced
2 bay leaves
1 carrot, cut up
Pinch salt substitute
4 peppercorns
Cook until done. Strain. Add a little of the fish liquid. Pour over fish and bake about 35 minutes, basting frequently. Sprinkle with paprika and a little chopped chervil and basil. Serve in same dish. (This is a basic rule and can be used for halibut, or haddock steak, etc.)

BAKED HADDOCK

Prepare a whole haddock with head and tail removed. Make stuffing, as for poultry, of bread crumbs, onion, celery leaves, 1 tsp. chopped parsley and chervil, half a bay leaf crumbled; moisten with melted butter and water. Spread this thickly over bottom half and fold top over and bake in medium oven.

BAKED FRESH
MACKEREL

Butter a pan well and lay a split fish skin side down. Add butter, salt substitute and finely chopped parsley and basil. Put in oven, and when it begins to cook pour over it a little white wine.

Baste often until done. Spread a few lacy leaves of chervil over the top when you serve it.

SEAFOOD SOUFFLE   Take two cups cooked and cut up seafood (may be crab meat, white fish, scallops, canned shrimp or lobster). Make 2 cups thick white sauce to which is added 2 Tb. finely chopped onion, 2 Tb. green pepper, a few dill seeds and a pinch of basil. Add 2 egg yolks beaten until light. Combine with fish. Fold in egg whites beaten stiff but not dry. Put in well-buttered casserole and bake 30 minutes in slow oven. Serve at once.

FILLETS OF SOLE, SCROD OR OTHER WHITE MEAT FISH   Wash four or five fillets of fish in lemon juice and water. Dry them on a cloth, place in lightly greased pyrex dish. Flavor with bay leaf, 1 or 2 peppercorns, few leaves of dill and a few small pieces of thyme. Pour over fish ½ cup water, 3 or 4 Tb. sherry and ½ cup white wine. Cover with waxed paper and bake 15 minutes in oven at 350°. Remove and serve at once.

CLAM CHOWDER
½ cup chopped onion
½ cup sliced celery
2 Tb. minced green pepper
2 Tb. margarine or butter
2 cups diced potatoes
2 cups boiling water
1½ tsp. salt
2 cans minced clams (7 oz.)
1 can (18 oz.) tomato juice
1 tsp. ground sage leaves
½ tsp. ground thyme leaves
¼ tsp. ground black pepper
Pinch tsp. ground cayenne pepper
1 tsp. paprika

Saute onion, celery and green pepper in margarine or butter in a saucepan large enough for making the soup. Add potatoes, boiling water and salt, cover. Cook until potatoes are tender, add remaining ingredients. Heat to boiling point. Serve in soup bowls over whole or crumbled crackers. Serves six.

FILLET ROLL-UPS
HERB STUFFING

4 fish fillets (flounder, haddock, etc.)
3 Tb. melted butter
1 Tb. lemon juice
½ tsp. salt or kelp
2 tsp. dried parsley flakes

⅛ tsp. paprika
1 tsp. crushed basil
¼ tsp. crumbled dried dill or dill seeds
1 Tb. minced onion
1 cup soft bread crumbs
2 Tb. melted butter

Combine 3 Tb. butter, lemon juice and seasonings. Add to bread crumbs, tossing with fork. Place stuffing on fillets. Roll up and fasten with toothpicks or tie with string. Place remaining butter and ½ tsp. basil in bottom of baking dish. Arrange fillets in pan. Bake in hot oven (400°) 25 to 30 minutes, basting several times with butter in pan. Serves four.

BAKED FISH

1 lb. white fish
⅓ cup butter or margarine
⅛ tsp. thyme
Sprigs of fresh dill and lovage

1 Tb. diced pimento
¼ tsp. paprika
¼ tsp. crushed celery seed
⅛ tsp. crushed fennel seed

Bake in casserole at 400° temperature.

Herb Jellies

BASIC HERB JELLY

One handful or ½ cup of your choice of herb
3 cups brown sugar
⅓ to ½ cup lemon juice or the juice of 2 lemons (grated peels may be used with herb)
½ cup liquid pectin
Few drops, green, yellow, orange, red vegetable color

Simmer a handful of herb for 10 to 15 minutes in a cupful of hot water. Keep covered to prevent loss of steam fragrance. Let stand 15 minutes and strain. Add enough warm water to fill the cup.

Add lemon juice and sugar and boil briskly ½ minute. Add the pectin and color and boil again ½ minute. Skim if necessary and pour into hot sterilized glasses. Cover with melted paraffin at once. Or boil the herbs in an apple jelly base for 2 minutes, remove and seal.

From store-bought Concord and the wild species of grape we have prepared sauces, jellies, and marmalades combined with herbs, lemon and orange peels. Grape wine is an excellent base with which to prepare an herb wine to be used to flavor cooked meats and as a wine sauce.

SPICED WILD
GRAPE JELLY

1 peck wild grapes, not quite ripe
1 quart cider vinegar, not too strong
½ cup whole pickling spices (cinnamon, cloves, etc.)
12 cups brown sugar

The grapes may or may not be separated from the stems. Add the spices (tied in a bag) and the vinegar, and cook until soft. Strain through a jelly bag. Boil the juice 20 minutes, add the sugar, which, to facilitate dissolving in the liquid, has been heated in the oven, and boil until the jelly stage is reached. Pour into sterilized glasses and cover with paraffin.

HERB WILD
GRAPE JELLY

To make thyme-flavored grape jelly, tie 2 teaspoons of dried thyme or a small bunch of fresh thyme in a cheesecloth bag, and add it to the grape juice before boiling. Remove it before adding the sugar. Very good with pork and game.

THE JELLY PULP

The pulp in the jelly bag may be used to make very appetizing jams and butters, good for spreading on the children's bread, for filling tarts, for making steamed and baked puddings, and for many other purposes.

HERB WINE
JELLY I

2¼ cups wine
3 cups sugar
½ bottle liquid pectin
Herbs: 1 tsp. each of summer savory, basil, thyme, to 1½ cups of white wine or ½ tsp. each oregano and marjoram to ½ cup red wine.
(General rule = ½ tsp. of herb to ½ cup wine.)
Slowly simmer herbs in warmed wine for 4 to 5 minutes. Strain into top of double boiler and

add sugar. Place over rapidly boiling water and stir sugar until dissolved. Remove from heat and immediately stir in pectin. Pour quickly into glasses and skim if necessary. Cover at once with ⅛ inch of hot paraffin wax. Makes 5 to 6 glasses.

HERB WINE
JELLY II

One or two Tb. rosemary or marjoram (or other herbs of your choice), 3 cups sugar and 2 cups sherry or sauterne wine.

Place the ingredients in a double boiler. Mix them well and prepare.

Uses of Herb Jelly

Herb	Cheese	Meat	Fish	Dessert	Eggs
Basil	x	x	x	x	
Fennel	x		x		x
Lemon verbena		x	x	x	x
Marjoram		x	x		
Mints	x	x	x	x	x
Rosemary		x	x		x
Sage		x	x		
Savory		x	x		
Tangerine (rinds)	x	x	x		
Tarragon		x	x		
Thyme	x	x	x		x

Herb Wines

These recipes are not intended to set up the neophyte herbalist in competition with the commercial wine producers; they are an introduction to another delightful use of herbs and another means of economizing in these times of rocketing prices. Any of the herb wines (or beers) may be used in wine cookery, as a seasoning and in the preparation of a wine jelly. When preparing a wine sauce or jelly, add an ounce of your herb wine to each six ounces of the desired product. Herb wines lead also to the manufacture of herb vinegars.

The proper management of the fermentation process contains the secret of the art of wine-making. Thus while many recipes for herb wines needlessly call for the addition of commercial wines or a stronger liquor, a properly controlled fermentation produces 5 to 8 per cent alcohol, enough to satisfy the requirements of any recipe. Commercial wines contain 10 to 20 per cent alcohol and their applications are discussed later.

The dishes that are prepared with herb wines taste of the particular aromatic herbs which flavor the wine. The alcoholic content of herb wines evaporates in the cooking process.

The difference between an herb wine and herb beer is that more aromatic flavoring is used in wine. A small amount of herbs is used in beer and there is the added ingredient of hops (and sometimes malt).

INGREDIENTS   The native herbs: angelica stems and roots, sweet birch, burdock herb, coltsfoot, currants, dandelion herb, yellow dock herb, elder fruits, sweet flag, gentian, gooseberries, wild grapes, horehound, nettle herb, yarrow and wormwood (herb here means the entire above ground portion, stem, leaves and flowers).

The culinary herbs: burnet, cardamon, coriander, lemon rind, marigold, marjoram, orange rind, rosemary, sage, and tangerine rind.

The spices: cinnamon, clove, ginger, mace, and nutmeg.

Note: When sugar is indicated in a recipe do use raw brown sugar or molasses. And for water it is best to use rain or distilled water. For beer, tap water is permissible.

HERB WINE   2 oz. dandelion herb
1 oz. yellow dock
1 oz. chamomile and nettle
1 oz. burdock
1 Tb. sassafras bark
1 Tb. ginger
3 lbs. sugar
    Boil the herbs for 15 to 20 minutes in a gallon of hot water. Strain the liquid and dissolve the sugar in it. Let stand a day stirring occasionally. Add another gallon of warm water, mix in an

ounce of yeast and allow to ferment about a week. Strain and bottle.

NATIVE HERB
WINE

2 pints nettle leaves   1 yeast cake
1 pint dandelion leaves   1½ to 2 lbs. brown su-
1 pint burdock leaves   gar
Rinds of 3 lemons   1½ gallons warm water
Peels of 5 oranges   1 oz. whole ginger
Peels of 7 tangerines

Simmer about one hour, stir well and let stand 10 to 14 days. For wine: Stir, strain, and bottle. Keep refrigerated. For vinegar: Omit ginger. After straining, let stand as before another 7–10 days.

JUNIPER BERRY
WINE

3 gallons water
3 quarts raisins
2 quarts juniper berries
⅓ handful wormwood
⅓ handful marjoram

Bring the water to a quick boil, add the other ingredients and allow to ferment 10 to 12 days.

ELDERBERRY
WINE

2 quarts elderberries
3 pounds sugar
1 pound raisins
1 ounce sweet flag root
  (or cinnamon, or ginger, ¼ oz.)
1 gallon water

Crush the ripe fruit. Boil in a gallon of water for one hour. Add the sugar and the spice. Boil again for ½ hour and set aside for 3 days. Add one pound of yellow raisins to each gallon. Let it stand for 60 days. Filter if so desired.

PRIMROSE WINE

1¾ lb. sugar
½ gallon water
½ gallon primrose flowers
  (or your favorite flowers)
Rind and juice of 1 lemon
Rind and juice of 1 orange

Water and sugar should be boiled together for half an hour. Add lemon and orange rinds and juice. When cool add primrose flowers. The liquor should stand in a warm place 7 days to ferment. Strain well. Pour into stone jar or other strong container, well corked. After four or five months, re-open and bottle.

BLUEBERRY WINE
2 gallons rain or boiled water
2 gallons cider
2 quarts blueberries
4 pounds brown sugar
1 ounce ginger
½ oz. lavender
½ oz. rosemary

Boil the water, add the herbs and the sugar. Allow to ferment a few days, strain and add the cider.

HERB BEER
One oz. each of: chamomile, sweet flag, horehound, hops, marjoram and sage
One gallon boiling water
½ pound malt
2 pounds sugar
1 pound raisins
1 yeast cake (1 oz.)

Boil the herbs and the malt in the water for 10 minutes and slowly simmer another hour. Strain and add the sugar and yeast. Allow to set one week. Strain and bottle.

HERB-ROOT BEER
1½ gallons water
2 pounds sugar
1 oz. each of: birch bark or twigs, burdock, dandelion, yellow dock, marjoram, sage, sarsaparilla and sassafras
1 yeast cake (1 oz.)

Boil the herbs in the water for 20 minutes, add the yeast cake and sugar, and allow to cool. Allow to ferment 5 or 6 days, strain and bottle. Keep in a cool place.

Using Herbed Wines

Although almost any of your favorite wines may be used with any food, it is suggested by some chefs that certain wines have an affinity for certain dishes. As well, there are taste harmonies between foods and commercial and home-made wines.

For example:

SHERRY   Appetizers, sauces, soups and stews. Fruits, pudding and meat sauce. To a cream soup add ⅓ Tb. of sherry to each cup.

SAUTERNE AND DRY WHITE WINES   Cheese dishes; chicken and fowl, fish and sea foods, lamb, veal.

BURGUNDY AND OTHER DRY RED WINES   Coarser meat cuts as chops, roasts, and steaks. Stuffings.

PORT AND MUSCATEL   Cookies, desserts, fruit jello and jelly molds.

You may use herbs and wine separately. It is not essential to refer to recipes in herb-wine cookery. Cooking with wine is accomplished merely by adding a little of the liquid to the pot. Flavoring one's foods with wines is as easy and intriguing as seasoning with thyme or marjoram.

Here is a general quantitative guide to the seasoning of meats with herbs and wines:

4 LB. CHICKEN   Half teaspoonful each of summer savory, basil and thyme, 1½ cups of dry white wine or sauterne.

4 LB. ROAST POULTRY   Half teaspoonful each of thyme, oregano, or marjoram. Half cup of burgundy or other dry red wine.

2 LB. VEAL   Quarter teaspoonful of herb in a cup of wine.

1½ LB. LAMB   Half teaspoonful each of thyme and marjoram. Two cups of rhine wine.

2 LB. BEEF   Half teaspoonful of marjoram and summer savory. Half cup of sherry. ¼ tsp. rosemary, ½ tsp. basil, ½ tsp. oregano. 1 cup red burgundy or red claret.

4 LB. ROAST   ¼ teaspoonful oregano; basil. One cup of red burgundy or claret.

1½ LB. LIVER   Half teaspoonful of thyme. 1 cup of sauterne or sherry.

Gently simmer the herbs in the required wine before using. An herb wine is excellent as a baste or marinade to flavor and tenderize various cuts of meats, especially wild game and fish. The food is generally marinated for 2 to 24 hours.

HERB BARBECUE   ½ cup sherry
WINE SAUCE   ¼ cup salad oil
                 1 medium sized onion, grated
                 1½ tsp. Worcestershire sauce
                 1 tsp. dry mustard
                 1½ tsp. mixed fresh herbs or thyme, marjoram,
                    rosemary or oregano
                 ½ tsp. garlic powder
                 ¼ tsp. vegetized salt or ½ tsp. kelp
                 Combine all ingredients in jar or bowl. Shake
                 or mix well before using. Enough for six servings.
                 (Excellent for marinating or basting beef, veal,
                 lamb, or chicken.)
                 Note: In the preparation of your favorite Herb
                 Sauce include ⅓ tsp. each of marjoram, rosemary,
                 or thyme or ½ tsp. each of basil and thyme to a
                 cup of burgundy or sauterne wine.

I do not encourage the use of wine as a beverage; as a culinary
aid it is permissible. Nor should wine be used as a "tonic" to
promote the appetite and enhance digestion. If appetite is lack-
ing and there is a problem of digestion, the solution would be a
temporary abstinence from all foods. A tisane of an aromatic
herb could be served as a temporary thirst-quencher and correc-
tive for the digestive system.

Herb flavorings for commercial wines include:

Angelica	Sweet flag	Peppermint
Lemon balm	Ginger	Rosemary
Basil	Juniper berries	Sage
Cardamon seeds	Lemon peel	Summer savory
Chamomile	Mace	Spearmint
Cinnamon	Marjoram	Tangerine peel
Cloves	Orange peel	Thyme
Currants	Oregano	Woodruff
Curry		

Sherry wine requires the sweeter herbs and mild spices.

Claret and burgundy require the stronger herbs and medium spices.

Sauterne and sweet wines require the pungent spices.

Herbed commercial wines may also be prepared by simply steeping the aromatic herb(s) in white wine for 3–4 days. Cover and allow the mixture to remain in a warm place, as in the preparation of an herb vinegar. Stir it daily. Strain through absorbent cotton or filter paper and bottle. Label the ingredients.

Herb Vinegars

There are some health enthusiasts who advocate the use of certain food products as "cure-alls," and who go a bit overboard in their claims for the virtues of their respective "wonder-foods." One such "food" is cider vinegar, and it has been the subject of exaggerated claims and praises. Not only does a diet of vinegar taken three or four times a day do harm to the user; it surrounds him with a tottering wall built of promises which cannot be fulfilled. The same criticism applies to other "cure-alls," such as honey and blackstrap molasses, yogurt, "high proteins," rose hips, wheat germ, milk products and sea-weed concentrates.

I see no harm in using herb vinegars for meat or fish sauce, and to flavor vegetables, salads and other foods. But to partake solely of vinegar and in frequent doses is to invite decided interference with the delicate balance of the gastric juices.

Cider vinegar, simply because it is made from apples, which are indeed good fruits to eat at all times, has been advertised to be rich in minerals and, therefore, especially healthy. It is supposed to help the drinker of that product in a number of ways: to reduce weight rapidly, prevent intestinal putrefaction, regulate metabolism, retard the onset of old age and promote digestion. Furthermore I have known it claimed that cider vinegar is good in the treatment of such ailments as stuffy nose, sore throat, cough, asthma, food poisoning, diarrhea, heart-burn, hiccoughs, joint diseases, insomnia and poor hair and nails. When combined with honey, it has been recommended as an effective remedy in the treatment of hay-fever, various heart troubles, colitis, arthritis and neuritis. Why, I ask, stop there? Many people read about a cider "cure-all," and being troubled with indigestion or colitis, hurry out to the market and begin dosing themselves with vinegar. The result—a more severe condition of indigestion and a "super" colitis.

Take a little of any vinegar, be it of the malt or cider variety, not as a food or food substitute, but as an ingredient in herbal seasoning. If you want the benefits of the apple, eat one in the morning or between meals. (Or make apple sauce seasoned with anise, dill or caraway seeds.)

The household making of vinegar infusions is practical. You may add to a vinegar some of the lemon, orange, or tangerine peels that you've dried during the spring and summer, and you may also add the leafless twig-ends of marjoram, rosemary, sage and tarragon, which are ordinarily discarded as waste after the last collection of the leaves in the fall, thus conserving all of the results of your labor in the garden. Certain herbs, as burnet and tarragon, lose some of their aromatic oil content upon drying, and placing them in vinegar presents a satisfactory means of preserving their desirable flavors in a stable solution.

The virtues of vinegar as a seasoning agent are well known. An herb vinegar will add unique flavor to salads, salad-dressings and many sauces. The vinegar affords an excellent opportunity to enjoy the subtlety of a particular herb flavor.

Let your taste buds be your judge of which herbs to use in vinegar. Use one or a combination of herbs. They may be herbs of a recent collection or from last year's crop. Remember, when combining your favorites with the strongly accented basil, garlic or tarragon, the powerful herbs should be used sparingly, and preferably into individual vinegars. Do prepare various combinations of either all cultivated herbs or, if you possess a streak of Yankee ingenuity, some cultivated and some found growing wild.

A few examples of suitable herbs for vinegar are basil, burnet, chives, dill, marjoram, rosemary, savory, tarragon and thyme. Among native herbs use allspice, bayberry, sweet birch, sweet flag, garlic, horseradish, juniper, mint, peppergrass, sassafras, tansy and wormwood. Don't overlook the possibility of vinegaring the rinds of lemon, orange and tangerine, and members of the onion family. Years ago, vinegared rose petals and elder flowers were considered dinner table delicacies.

Either wine, cider or malt vinegar may be used to create a most satisfactory end product. If you are to practice the fine art of seasoning with wine vinegar, be sure your basis is a dry white wine, sauterne or claret. Since such vinegars are often hard to find commercially, I suggest substituting any of the other two.

BASIC HERB VINEGAR

Ingredients: 2–3 heaping cups of herbs, collected before flowering (½ to 1 cup if dried herbs are used); one quart vinegar (warmed).

Directions: Combine the herb with the vinegar and pack the jars lightly but as full as possible to exclude air. Let stand in a warm place for two weeks. Strain into clean bottles. Label.

MINT VINEGAR

Ingredients: 3 cups fresh peppermint leaves; 1 quart cider vinegar; 1 cup brown sugar.

Directions: Bring the vinegar to a quick boil. Add the mint and sugar, and simmer gently for another four to five minutes. Strain into clean, warmed bottles. If you wish, omit the sugar, and prepare as under "Basic Herb Vinegar."

AROMATIC VINEGAR

1 gallon cider vinegar, 1 oz. each of dill seed, lavender flowers, rue, spearmint, rosemary, sage, wormwood. Let stand in an earthen jar in a warm place.

GARLIC AND SPICE VINEGAR

6 cloves garlic (minced)	Nutmeg (crushed)
6 whole cloves	Juice of 4 lemons
Basil	1 qt. vinegar

Boil and steep two to three weeks.

CELERY VINEGAR

1 qt. vinegar	1 lb. chopped celery
½ oz. celery seed (crushed)	2 tsp. brown sugar
	1 tsp. salt substitute

Heat vinegar (being careful *not* to boil) with the crushed celery seed, salt and sugar to nearly simmering, pour over the chopped celery and allow to cool. Pour the mixture into a large bottle and shake it well each day for 12 to 14 days. Then strain, cool, cork and store it until needed for use.

SALAD VINEGAR

A very good salad vinegar can be made of a mixture of 3 ounces each of tarragon, basil, and shallots, a handful of the tops of peppermint and lemon peel, all dried and pounded, 2 crushed cloves of garlic. Use one gallon of vinegar. Put into wide-mouthed bottle and let stand for a month, shaking or stirring daily. Then press all the juice and vinegar from the herbs. Let stand a day to settle, then strain through flannel bag. Bottle and seal.

COMPOUND
TARRAGON
VINEGAR

Take 3 ounces each of tarragon, savory, chives, shallots, a handful of dry and pounded mint and balm; put into wide-mouth bottle with a gallon of vinegar; cork it; set in the sun for two weeks, strain off and squeeze the herbs; let it stand a day to settle and then strain it through a filtering bag.

NATIVE
HERB-SPICE
VINEGAR

Use wild allspice, bayberry leaves, sweet flag roots, wild garlic, horseradish roots, sassafras bark, and early tansy leaves, and one quart of cider or native wine vinegar:

Bring the vinegar to the boiling point. Add a tablespoonful each of the wild allspice, bayberry, sweet flag, sassafras and tansy, all ground, and a teaspoonful each of the minced garlic and grated horseradish. Stir the herbs and simmer gently for 10 minutes. Cover and allow to cool. Let stand two weeks in a warm place. Stir and strain. Bottle and label.

The purpose of an herb vinegar is to add zest to a salad or sauce. But use discretion. It is far better to add a very few drops of your favorite herb vinegar to your food, for too many will invite gastric disturbances.

For everyday use, malt and cider vinegars will suffice admirably, and after experimenting with each you can decide which you like best. Never use distilled white vinegar. The practical herbalist, always a conservationist, will prepare his own vinegar, employing native (weed-like) herbal plants. Here is one of my "secret formulas" for preparing a typical herb beer or wine, which upon further fermentation, yields the acetic acid to develop vinegar.

NATIVE HERB
WINE VINEGAR

3 cupfuls of nettle leaves, one cup of burdock, one cup of dandelion leaves; the rinds of 3 lemons, 5 oranges, and 5 tangerines; a yeast cake, 1½–2 pounds of brown sugar, and 1½ gallons of hot water. (If to prepare the wine only, add one ounce of whole ginger or wild ginger).

Simmer the mixture about an hour, stirring occasionally. Cover and let stand 10–14 days in a wide mouthed crock.

If the product is intended as a wine, stir, strain the liquid first through cheesecloth and immediately pass it through filter paper. Label the bottles and refrigerate them.

To prepare the vinegar, return the strained solution to the crock and allow it to ferment another 7–10 days.

Create your own epicurean herb vinegars but at all times practice sensible moderation. In salads, use herb vinegar with safflower, soy bean or peanut oil. Be careful with garlic and tarragon vinegar, because each can overpower the delicate flavor of the food. The sensible user of vinegar will accent a favorite sauce or salad dressing—and have better digestion.

MISCELLANEOUS USES OF VINEGAR   Marinating with herb vinegar is an old culinary trick. The vinegar acts as a gentle "tenderizer" for meats, fowl and venison. The acidity is dissipated with heat but the herbal taste lingers on.

STEAK OR CHOP
MARINADE

Steaks or chops are tenderized by marinating with any desired vinegar before frying or broiling. (Try basil vinegar as a starter.) Put 1 Tb. of vinegar in a shallow plate and twist the uncooked meat around it, making sure that the entire outside is moistened with the vinegar.

POT ROAST OR
STEW MEAT
MARINADE

Pot roasts or stew meats are tenderized and vastly improved in flavor when given this marinating treatment: Mix ⅓ cup of desired vinegar, 1 cup of broth or water and ⅓ cup of oil. Put meat in bowl, pour on liquid. Let stand from 3 to 12 hours, turning from time to time for uniform marinating. (The longer the better; however, even a few hours works wonders.)

AROMATIC
VINEGAR

Place one level teaspoon each of clove, ginger, cinnamon, sassafras, lemon peel and orange peel in 8 ounces of cider vinegar. Steep for 10 days, stirring occasionally. Then stir, strain and add enough vinegar to measure 8 ounces (to replace what has evaporated).

If this preparation is intended for external use only, add instead 8 ounces of alcohol in which ½ ounce of camphor has been dissolved. This aromatic vinegar should be applied externally to insect bites or stings and to scratches and bruises.

VINEGAR GARGLE

1 part (or ounce) sage vinegar
4 parts honey
4 parts (optional) barley water
  Mix and gargle every hour. The barley water must be freshly prepared by steeping a teaspoonful of unpearled barley in a cup of hot water.

VINEGAR
LINIMENT

2 oz. tarragon, tansy or 1 tsp. ground red
   wormwood vinegar   pepper
3 oz. turpentine   1 tsp. ground ginger
3 oz. witch hazel   1 tsp. ground cloves
  Mix the liquids. Allow the spices to stand in the liquid for 3 or 4 days, and keep in a warm place. Stir and strain.

VINEGAR HAIR
APPLICATION

To keep hair bright and ward off grey: rub, a little at a time, rosemary or sage vinegar onto the hair.

VINEGAR   1 part thyme vinegar
POULTICE   3 parts corn starch
            Mix well and apply to affected area. Serves
well as an astringent and antiseptic application.

Herb Marinades

To marinate is to cold-baste food with a liquid before cooking. Marinating is a modern version of the ancient rite of animal sacrifice. In those days the animal was slaughtered and then soaked in home-made wine and aromatic herbs and spices. After a specified time of such steeping, the animal was "barbecued."

To marinate or not is a question of personal taste. There is no end to the combinations of herbs and liquids which can be used. Indeed, the more adventuresome cook may want to use the leaves, fruits and other aromatic parts of wild-growing plants: juniper berries, sassafras bark, the various mints, catnip and bayberry leaves, wild allspice and peppergrass fruits, and of course, grape leaves, to name several.

A marinade softens coarse meats and game and fish, and reduces harmful fat of such food. At the same time, the meats are temptingly perfumed and improved in taste. In many cases stomach disorders are prevented since obnoxious stomach toxins are well counteracted by the marination.

A marinade becomes a hot basting solution when so needed, as well as a pre-seasoned gravy or sauce. The left-over sauce may be saved and re-warmed when needed to serve as a sauce for other meats. Many chefs of high-priced restaurants use the technique of marinating of foods for some 8–10 hours over a low heat, turning over and basting the food once an hour or so.

Generally, herb marinated foods need no further flavoring when served—no salt, no pickles, no relish.

The ingredients of a marinade are the liquids: lemon juice, vermouth or other dry or white wine (unless otherwise specified), olive or other vegetable oil, cider vinegar, herb vinegar of your choice, and chicken stock; and the seasonings: basil, caraway, chervil, chives, dill seeds or leaves, fennel, garlic, juniper berries, marjoram, onion, oregano, parsley, rosemary, sage, savory, tarragon, thyme and the dried rinds of lemons, limes, oranges and tangerines. Wild grape leaves and cabbage leaves are often used with deer, hare, pheasant or quail.

BASIC MARINADE	¼ cup oil	1 large onion chopped
	1½–2 cups dry wine	1 clove garlic chopped
	(or vermouth)	1 Tb. parsley chopped
	1 or 2 tsp. lemon juice	1 Tb. celery tops or
	2 Tb. herb vinegar	chervil
	½ tsp. herbs (optional)	Try to do without
		salt or pepper

FISH   Take 2 lb. tuna, sea bass, mackerel, cod or snapper. When using a whole fish, remove the head and tail and halve lengthwise. Remove all bones. Prepare a marinade of above quantities of white wine, herb vinegar, onion and garlic (or garlic vinegar), 2 tsp. of either lime or lemon juice and its rind grated or cut into very thin pieces, and ½ tsp. of a mixture of basil, marjoram, coarsely ground fennel, tarragon or thyme (or of any one).

Warm the pan containing the fish and the liquids, and other ingredients. Top the fish with 1 Tb. parsley or celery leaves and heat for ½ hour or so. Refrigerate for 10–12 hours before serving. Turn the fish over every other hour.

Marinated fish is often served as an appetizer. It is equally good as the main course and can be gently warmed.

MEATS   For any beef, even a prime rib roast, mix vegetable oil, herb vinegar or lemon juice, wine, chopped Bermuda onion and the garlic, marjoram, rosemary and parsley.

Make incisions between ribs and rub in the marinade. Then roll in waxed paper and refrigerate for one full day (24 hours). Before cooking, remove the waxed paper. Brush the meat with more oil and the marinade and heat 2 to 2½ hours at 250–300°.

No basting is needed and there is very little shrinkage.

The marinade encourages the meat juices to develop as a pre-seasoned gravy. Save left-over gravy in the refrigerator for future use.

For pot roast, treat with marinade as indicated but do not make incisions. Use extra pieces of onions and parsley on the meat at temperature indicated above.

For pork, the marinade includes onions, garlic, shallots, leeks or chives, parsley, thyme, basil or marjoram, vegetable oil and lemon juice and ground rinds.

Make usual incisions and heat at 250°. Cook ½ hour for each pound or until pink is gone.

For a 3-lb. steak 1¼ inch thick mix 1 cup oil, 4 oz. each vinegar and wine (sherry or vermouth), ½ Tb. each rosemary and basil or oregano, juice of a lemon and the ground rind, a cupful chopped parsley, 2 large Bermuda onions, 2 cloves garlic chopped fine. Pour over and rub into the meat. Let this marinate overnight. Broil according to your taste.

For lamb, the marinade includes the usual ingredients and the seasoning herbs of marjoram, thyme, caraway and an extra amount of parsley. Remove the excess fat. Make the usual incisions and marinate as above. Refrigerate the marinated lamb for 24 hours in waxed paper. Lamb chops are marinated 6–8 hours before broiling. Lamb intended for a *ragout* or stewed lamb should remain in the marinade for 12 to 14 hours.

For veal, use the usual marinade ingredients, but veal is bland so add more parsley (a cupful); ½ to 1 Tb. juniper berries, if obtainable, 1 tsp. thyme, shallots and the juice of a lemon plus the rind. Allow veal to marinate 24 hours before heating.

A marinade will invariably flavor turkey or chicken better than any stuffing.

For poultry (prepared chicken, duck, goose, squab and turkey), the marinade is composed of lemon juice (optional), onions and garlic (or related leeks and chives), and thyme and rosemary.

For turkey, prepare as usual, allow to marinate 24 hours. If the turkey is to be stuffed, the marinade should be removed. To season the stuffing, add marjoram or oregano, savory and sage, and if possible, fresh chervil and parsley.

For goose, prepare as with turkey. If a gosling, use usual amounts of liquids plus parsley, chives and leeks, marjoram or rosemary.

For duck, season the marinade with rosemary, tarragon, caraway seeds, parsley, chervil, onion and garlic. Marinate 24 hours. If the bird is to be stuffed, do not marinate, do use the herbs as part of the stuffing.

For chicken, use the usual ingredients and season with marjoram and thyme, and all greens, leeks and shallots, and the like. Marinate 12 hours.

For capon, prepare as with chicken. Season with juniper berries and rosemary.

For squab, prepare as with chicken. Use fresh parsley and celery leaves and a little extra herb seasoning.

For game (quail, pheasant, partridge, deer, et al), use large leaves of grapes and cabbage. Prepare the usual marinade of liquids (wine, vinegar, oil and lemon juice), add vegetables and seasoning herbs of juniper berries, thyme, oregano and rosemary. Allow to marinate 48 hours.

For hare (not rabbit), prepare as indicated under game. Add chopped chervil, leeks or shallots. Season with your choice of juniper berries, rosemary, basil, oregano or marjoram.

Marinate mushrooms in your favorite herb vinegar for several days. You will then not have to cook them and you will save time and what little food value mushrooms have to offer. Marinated mushrooms so prepared may be served as appetizers.

Canning with Herbs

The preservation of native fruits in jellies or jams is a profitable practice. The surplus produce of one's vegetable garden can also be practically and profitably preserved by canning and a large variety of vegetables and fruits thus shall be made available during the winter months. However, nature's wildings (the edible herbs) which are always in abundance, unsprayed with chemical poisons, and replete with healthy nutrients are most effectively preserved by dehydration—drying. But, there are many worth-while reasons for using culinaries in the canning of vegetables. They will generally improve the taste of bland roots and vegetables. It can add appeal to those foods which one does not particularly enjoy but which are important for nutrition.

I conducted a survey concerning various dietary habits in 1951 through my radio program and learned that 80% of the housewives interviewed who practiced canning did not employ herbs. The one exception was, of course, the preparation of pickles, which included the beneficial herbs, dill and garlic.

Although canning has obvious advantages—economy, conservation of healthy foods which are plentiful in summer and the convenience of vegetables at arm's reach during the winter —remember that canned foods are inferior in flavor and composition to their natural counterparts, and should never be substituted for the fresh or unprocessed article. The advantages, especially in areas where fresh produce is not easily or economically obtainable during the winter months, outweigh this disadvantage.

The canner should experiment with the preserving of wild crab-apples, rose-hips, grapes and other wild fruits, and save orange and lemon rinds in jams or marmalade. By drying the excess radish, turnip, and beet leaves, early dandelion and lambs-quarters greens, as well as the summer's blueberries and raspberries, one will have a source of edible, dry (preserved) foodstuff that is more economical and of greater benefit to one's health than the "boiling to spoiling" method. To prepare any such summer-dried product, one should gently steam a portion in the least amount of water. Do not use the pressure cooker. To stimulate the gustatories, one should usually add a few drops of a favorite herb vinegar or lemon juice to the dried greens.

The art of cooking or preserving foods with herbs is an art of variety. Both the novice and experienced cook will truly marvel at the results gained by the addition of a sprig or two of a given herb to accent the appeal of many vegetables.

Do not add herbs to the food while it is in the cooking stage.

Always season by adding a sprig or a substantial pinch of herbs to each jar just before bottling or capping. One exception to the general rule is flavoring rhubarb with angelica, which is cooked with the rhubarb.

If you are to put up peas or beans, collect them before they are mature. An overstock of early beets or carrots may be preserved in jars and eaten as is; if the carrots are large, they are first preserved and later diced or sliced.

Preserving Guide

Food	Herb (Your choice of one)
Apple (as is or the sauce)	Anise, Mint, Caraway, Dill
Beans (Lima, Soy, Mung, String)	Basil, Lovage, Sage, Summer Savory, Dill
Beets	Dill, Fennel, Garlic, Thyme
Carrots	Dill, Fennel, Thyme, Mint, Basil
Pears	Mint, Lemon Balm
Peas	Basil, Summer Savory, Mint
Rhubarb	Angelica stem or root (cooked with Rhubarb)
Squash	Angelica stem
Tomatoes	Basil, Oregano, Summer Savory
Turnips	Dill, Fennel, Tarragon, Lovage, Sage

Native Edibles	Herbs
Barberries	Mint, Anise
Burdock	Wild Allspice, Basil
Wild (skunk) Cabbage	(Wild) Onion, Caraway
Cat-tail (young shoots)	Lovage
Chickweed	(Wild) Garlic
Dandelion	Basil, Oregano, Savory
Lambsquarter	Basil, Oregano
Marsh-marigold Buds	Dill, Wild Allspice
Milkweed	Dill
Nettle	Basil, Summer Savory
Pokeweed	Basil, Sage, Savory
Purslane	Basil, Sage, Savory
Sorrel	Garlic, Oregano

Some authorities assert that each herb has a particular affinity with a given vegetable, and must be used only in that instance. For example, they insist that peas and carrots must be minted, beets and cucumbers be dilled, and beans must ever be matched with summer savory. But the use of herbs in any phase of cooking or preserving has always been a matter of personal choice, and for that reason there are no set rules for recipes. Experiment for yourself with more variety and you, too, will enjoy the difference between store-bought and home-made canned foods.

When "protein" beans are used, as lima, soy and mung, add such herbs as are intended to flavor meat, such as basil, sage and savory. Where the celery tang is desired, use a little lovage root—judiciously.

Recipes for vegetables (and also for stews and soups) often include chives and parsley. Remember that these two salad greens will lose most of their vitamin content in the process of heating; therefore always eat them raw and uncooked.

Tisanes

A tisane (also spelled ptisane and tizane) is an herb tea generally intended as a substitute for tea or coffee. It should be drunk by all and especially by those who may be affected by the dyspepsia-inducing tannic acid in tea and the insidious and harmful over-stimulation of the caffeine in coffee.

A warm herb tea will keep one cool in the summer and more comfortable in the winter time. Those who like a refresher or a mildly aromatic after-dinner drink (to be taken one hour after or, better, between meals) will certainly derive much more comfort and pleasure from a "Northern Julep" of mint and sage than from pekoe tea.

The word tisane, from the Latin *ptisana* meaning barley water, is defined in the dictionary as a "nourishing decoction often having a slight medicinal quality." A simple herb infusion (tisane) will do more than boost drooping spirits like ordinary tea. Tisanes gently stimulate the processes of elimination, act benignly upon the glandular system and relax the nerves in a way superior to nicotine, drugs and caffeine. People who take herb teas are known to develop an inner calm.

Long before Chinese tea was introduced to the European countries, the common people enjoyed their refreshing drinks of balm, mint, and sage. I am encouraged by the many reports received from herb users who, having at long last abandoned the tea and coffee habit, echo what herbalist Gerard wrote in 1597: "If odours may worke satisfaction, they are so soveraigne in plants, and so comfortable, that no confection of the apothecaries can equal them in virtue." Naturalist Henry Thoreau described the aroma of his tea of sassafras: "that fragrance of lemons and a thousand spices." Others have considered teas of wintergreen "very refreshing and thirst-satisfying with a flavor like some rare perfume." A tea of chamomile "brings back pleasant memories of my childhood in the old country." Tisanes of linden and catnip "calm the nerves and avert the need for sleeping pills"; of lemon balm and mint "have remarkably improved my mental as well as physical health"; of mint and sweet clover are "an excellent stomach comforter," and so the reports run.

But how does the inveterate drinker of coffee or tea learn to partake of herb teas and, more important, to forsake the everyday harmful dietary habits which have been acquired over the years? If the tea or coffee drinker genuinely desires to turn tisanist and will gradually abandon those beverages, he must immediately abandon many associated dietary practices, such as eating fatty meats which are high in cholesterol and the overdosing of his often tasteless foods with the usual array of salt, vinegar, spices, ketchup and their confederates. He should also abandon the practice of drinking liquor before, wine with and liqueur after each meal. Eating fatty animal foods is stimulating. The use of salt and spices as food seasoners is stimulating. Smoking is stimulating. Will he abandon these habits or appreciably reduce them? How much more stimulation can the already enervated human system stand before the inevitable physical deterioration, resulting in more and more cases of nervousness and high blood pressure, kidney disorders, and various heart troubles? The elimination of such faulty habits will lead to better health, and to the enjoyment of the priceless aroma of chamomile and mint, or lemon balm and linden, and of other tisanes. Here is my suggested "course" which has been taken by many former meat-eaters, spice-users, heavy smokers and liquor drinkers:

First, prepare a cup of ordinary pekoe tea and add a whole clove or a small piece of cinnamon. This helps give the drink the "exotic" touch. Drink the tea one hour after meals, sipping it slowly. Try this for a week or so.

Then, prepare the tea using less pekoe. Add a few small pieces of dried orange peels and lemon peels or both (about ½ teaspoon of each), with or without the spices. Do this for a week.

Then, prepare the tea and now add ¼ teaspoon each of mint and a little sage or other herbal aromatics. Try this for 10–15 days, gradually reducing the amount of the pekoe tea.

Finally now prepare a tea only of the herbs. Herb teas now should include yarrow, mint, catnip, rosemary, sage, linden and chamomile.

PREPARATION OF TISANE   Always prepare a fresh cup of herb tea. Use only fresh tap or rain water. Rinse the cup and saucer with hot water before adding the herbs. Use china or glazed pottery, but not metal or aluminum.

Use dried herbs. One teaspoonful of dried equals one heaping tablespoonful of fresh undried herbs.

Steep, stir well (15–20) times, one teaspoonful of the herb in a cupful of hot water and cover with a saucer for 5–7 minutes. Stir and strain into a cup, previously warmed with hot water. The infusion must be almost tepid before it is drunk.*

* Other writers have stated that tisanes, during the warm, summer days, can be served cold or iced, but most practicing herbalists recommend that an herbal substitute for pekoe tea be drunk while still warm to tepid. Iced teas are therapeutically inert and unwholesome and therefore not recommended.

Do not add milk or cream, sugar or honey, or other sweetening agent. A few drops of the freshly expressed juice of a lemon may be added to the strained infusion to sharpen the flavor.

Do not eat at least one hour before or after drinking an herb tea. Above all, have your herb tea not so much as an after dinner beverage, as a replacement for tea or coffee, but as a thirst quencher and then only as needed between meals.

Do not drink hot tea—only lukewarm to tepid. Hot and cold liquids tend to destroy the food digesting enzymes.

Sip the infusion slowly, about 1 or 2 teaspoonsful at a time. Swish the tisane around in the mouth, there the better to mix with the primary digestive enzyme, so that the benefits of the infusion may be assimilated into the blood stream within an hour or two.

HERB TEA
COMBINATION
1. One part each of Rosemary, Rose Leaves (ground), Orange and Lemon Rinds. Teaspoonful to a cup of hot water.

2. One part each of Marjoram, Fennel, Mint or Catnip.

Herbs For Tisanes

Alfalfa	Fern, Sweet	Rose (wild) Leaves
Angelica	Goldenrod, Sweet	Rose Geranium
Anise	Hyssop	Rosemary
Balm, Lemon	Lavender	Sage
Basil	Lemon Rind	Sassafras
Bergamot, Red	Linden	Spearmint
Birch, Sweet	Marjoram	Strawberry, Wild
Caraway	Meadow Sweet	Sumac, Flowers and
Catnip	Mint, Garden	Early Fruit
Chamomile	New Jersey Tea	Tangerine Rind
Clover, Red	Orange Rind	Thyme
Clover, Sweet	Peppermint	Verbena, Lemon
Elder Flowers	Pine Leaves	Wintergreen
Fennel	Raspberry Leaves	Yarrow

Not recommended: Costmary, Rue, Tansy and Woodruff.

3. One part each of Yarrow, Sweet Fern, Basil.
4. One part each of Sage, Lemon Rind, Catnip, Mint.

Cough Remedies and Candy

Soothing syrups and lozenges to alleviate the irritation of a cough may be made from herbs. Here is a fine recipe for each.

HERBAL COUGH SYRUP

Anise Seed (or Mint)
Boneset Herb
Coltsfoot
Horehound
Hollyhock Root (or Mallow)
Mullein Leaf
Thyme

Use equal portions of any combination and mix. Slowly simmer an ounce of the mixture in a pint of boiling water for 20 minutes, the utensil being covered. Stir and strain. To each cupful of liquid add 1⅓ cups of sugar. Stir well until completely dissolved. Strain into a clean bottle and cover. The dose is a dessert spoonful sipped slowly, as often as is needed to allay irritation due to cough or cold.

Herbs	Uses
Alfalfa and Mint	Source of vitamins A, D, E, K, minerals Calcium, Iron, Manganese
Lemon Balm	Used to flavor fruit drinks
Chamomile	Calmative, digestant
Linden and Mint	Anti-dyspeptic
Catnip	Calmative in sleeplessness or nervousness
Catnip and Fennel	Carminative
Sage and Catnip	"Cold Breaker"
Sage and Peppermint	"Northern Julep"
Rose Petals	Source of vitamin C, minerals Magnesium, Calcium, Iron
Basil, Rosemary, Sage	To relieve headache
Checkerberry and Mint	"Anti-rheumatic"

HERBAL LOZENGES   Anise Seed
Black Currants
Coltsfoot
Horehound
Hollyhock Roots
Mallow, low or high
Marshmallow Roots
Mullein Leaves
Sassafras Bark
Thyme
2 cups of one or any mixture of herbs, freshly
     dried and ground
1 quart of boiling water
4–5 cups of brown sugar
Note: Use only a Tb. of either Anise, Currants, or
     Sassafras.

Boil the herbs briskly in the water about 10
minutes and simmer another 30 minutes. Stir well
and strain through cheesecloth. Add about 1½
cups of the sugar to each cupful of the strained
decoction and boil again. Stir until the solution
begins to thicken. The mixture is then poured
into a buttered pan and cut in squares, while it
is cooling. When the squares are dried dust them
with confectionery sugar.

When preparing a lozenge of anise or some
other aromatic herb, always first prepare a decoction of the non-aromatic herb of your choice,
mullein, boneset, or mallow, and then add the
aromatic when ready to simmer another 30 minutes. Keep the utensil covered.

CANDIED FLOWERS   Flowers: Rose, Borage, Violet, Cowslip.
AND LEAVES   Leaves: Peppermint, Spearmint, Sage, Lemon
Balm, Horehound.

Gather the largest leaves or flowers in the early
morning. Wash them in cold water and dry carefully. Add a half teaspoonful of water to one
egg white and whip. A thin solution of acacia
(gum arabic) may also be used (a teaspoonful of
the powder mixed with a cup of sugar and dissolved with hot water).

First dip both sides of the leaves in the egg white mixture (a tweezer may be used) and then in sugar or in the acacia-sugar solution. Allow to dry crisp on wax paper. When completely dry, place between sheets of wax paper and store in air-tight container.

The solution may also be painted onto the tender herbs with an artist's brush.

CANDIED ROOTS

Angelica
Elecampane
Sweet Flag
Ginger
Wild Ginger
Lovage
Marshmallow
Burdock
Chestnuts
Pith of Burdock

Use 4 or 5 roots. Mix 2 cups sugar and 2 cups water to prepare a syrup. To add extra flavor to the non-aromatic herbs—burdock, chestnuts or marshmallow—add a little (⅓–½ tsp.) of one or two culinaries, as anise, savory, marjoram or thyme.

Clean the freshly collected roots and allow to stay in cold water overnight. Cut into thin, transverse (cross) sections. Simmer the roots for 30 minutes in 2 cups of boiling water and stir occasionally. The roots remain in this decoction for about 3 to 4 hours. Strain and save this solution for further use. Simmer the roots again for 30 minutes in a syrup previously prepared. The root sections are removed when clean, thoroughly dried on waxed paper, and stored in air-tight containers.

Save both the decoction water and syrup which, when mixed with more (brown) sugar, afford one with a stable product which will contain the therapeutic benefits of the particular herb. For example, the remaining solution of angelica or ginger becomes a carminative or gas-expelling remedy, and that of elecampane and marshmallow, a mild expectorant for bronchial disorders.

WILD GINGER
CANDY

To candy these roots, just soak overnight in cold water, simmer for one hour to soften and then cook slowly in a heavy sugar syrup till the roots are entirely clear and soft. Dry on waxed paper and sprinkle with granulated sugar.

CANDIED ORANGE
PEEL

Choose thick peel from 4 fragrant California navel oranges. Soak peel overnight in salted water. Drain. Cover with cold water, bring to a boil. Drain. Repeat twice more, then simmer in fresh water until tender. Drain, cool, cut in narrow strips.

Make syrup of 1 cup sugar, ½ cup water and a pinch of salt. Add a 2-inch branch of tender, fragrant rosemary (not the resinous variety) and cook peel slowly until transparent. Let stand overnight in syrup. Drain. Coat with granulated sugar. A tender young 2-inch angelica stem may be used instead of the rosemary.

Herb Pillows

Whenever herb pillows are mentioned to me, I am reminded of a member of our Herb Club, who especially enjoyed making the fragrant herb pillows. One evening, he was to prepare herb teas for us and he searched in his workshop for suitable herbs among his huge stock of dried herb mixtures and liquid decoctions. But to his dismay, he was all out of tisane herbs. Without further delay he took two of his herb pillows, and from each he extracted enough chamomile and sweet fern to prepare the herbal refreshments.

If you want to make herb pillows, the essential herbs to be used are six—the leaves of sweet fern, bayberry, life everlasting, pine and sassafras, and the floss or silk of fall-maturing milkweed pod. If sleep is your intention, then add hops or lavender; if it is an aromatic pillow—an exaggerated sachet—then add a portion of lavender, marjoram, mint, rosemary, basil, rose petals and rose geranium leaves. Add any of your favorite culinary or sachet herbs.

Basic combinations are:

1. 1 part Bayberry, 1 part Sweet Fern
2. 3 parts Sweet Fern, 2 parts Bayberry, 1 part Sassafras
3. Sleep inducer: 1 part Bayberry, 2 parts Sweet Fern, 3 parts Hops
4. 3 parts Sweet Fern, 3 parts Hops, 2 parts Bayberry, 1 part Sassafras

To each of these combinations, 1 part of Lavender may be added.

Remove the coarse stems before inserting the herbs into the pillows.

Smaller sized fragrant pillows, 6 × 6 inches, may be placed over a warm radiator, for their aromas serve almost as well as deodorizers. They make excellent Christmas and birthday gifts.

An herb pillow (6 × 6) that can serve as a disinfectant is prepared by stuffing bags full of dried leaves of arbor vitae, plus an equal amount containing juniper, thyme and rosemary. When a sick room needs to be aired and disinfected, leave the windows open a while, then close them and place an arbor vitae bag on a warm radiator until the herb's aroma fills the room. Temper the rather strong essence by adding some of the more pleasant aromatics.

Sachets

It is easy to prepare your own sachets, or sweet bags as they are rightly called by some. Sachet is derived from the Latin word, *saccus,* a bag. They are usually kept in the dresser drawers, in linen closets and in or nearby one's everyday clothes, where the welcome fragrance of the aromatic herbs may diffuse throughout, offering delightful scents and acting as a deterrent to moths.

The following list of sachet herbs ranges from the conventional to the exotic. The latter category includes such ingredients as the dried, coarsely ground rinds of lemon, orange, and tangerine, the leaves of various household sweet geraniums and violets, and especially those wild sweet scented herbs as sweet clover, milk-weed flowers, and the anise-scented goldenrod. Novel ingredients for homemade sachets are the unopened flower heads of the lilac which are collected and thoroughly dried while yet on their stems.

If your taste is more toward the exotic, include these spices: allspice, cloves, nutmeg, cinnamon and mace.

As in the case of which culinaries to flavor one's foods, there is no particular combination, no set formula. Choose your favorites from among the culinaries and experiment with mixtures. Build your mixtures around such basic herbs as lavender, the mints, marjoram, rosemary, and rose buds or petals which should constitute at least one-third of the entire amount. Rose geranium, heliotrope, woodruff and bergamot may also be used. Be sure to add a generous sprinkle of ground florentine orris root, sweet flag or gum benzoin, which acts as a fixative.

Sachet suggestions:

1. 4 parts rose geranium or rose buds, 2 parts lavender, 1 part

Sachet Ingredients

Allspice	Hops	Rosemary
Lemon Balm	Lavender	Rue
Basil	Lemon (rind)	Sassafras (bark)
Red Bergamot	Lilac	Southernwood
Chamomile	Lily of the Valley	Spearmint
Cinnamon	(flowers)	Tangerine (rind)
Clove	Mace	Thyme
Yellow Clover	Marjoram	Tonka
White Clover	Milkweed (flowers)	Vanilla
Sweet Flag	Nutmeg	Lemon Verbena
Sweet Geranium	Oranges (rind)	Sweet Violets
Sweet-scented	Orris	Wintergreen
Goldenrod	Peppermint	Woodruff
Heliotrope (flowers)	Rose Buds	Wormwood

marjoram, plus smaller quantities of mint, chamomile and cloves.

2. 8 parts rose buds and petals, 4 parts lemon verbena, 2 parts cloves, 2 parts lavender, 2 parts milkweed flowers, 1 part thyme, and 1 part lilac.

3. 4 parts rose geranium, 4 parts rose buds, 1 part hops, ½ part cinnamon, ½ part sassafras, 1 part cloves.

The material for your sweet bags may be colored silk or cotton, discarded or torn blouses and shirts, and the like. The measurements are 2 by 4 inches. Or you may prefer the tri-cornered hat effect, with a 2 or 3 inch dimension. Insert 2 level tablespoonsful of your mixture into each bag and tighten with string or ribbon. Remember that your sachets also discourage moths and the finished sachet bags also may be hung over the backs of chairs, placed in the corners of upholstered seats and in closets.

SWEET BAG FOR LINEN I   Take a pound each of orris roots, sweet calamus, cypress-roots, dried lemon-peel and dried orange-peel and a peck of dried roses. Grind all these into a gross powder. Add 4 ounces of coriander-seed, an ounce and a half of nutmeg, an ounce of cloves, ground into a fine powder. Add 4 large handfuls of lavender flowers dried and rubbed, a handful each dried sweet marjoram, orange-leaves, and young walnut-leaves. Mix all the ingredients together, and put it up into silk bags to lay with your linen.

SWEET BAG FOR LINEN II   This sachet may be composed of any mixture of the following articles: Powdered cloves, mace, nutmeg, cinnamon; dried and pounded mint, balm, southernwort, ground-ivy, laurel, hyssop, sweet marjoram, oregano and rosemary leaves; cassia, juniper, sandal-wood, and angelica and orris roots.

Pot-Pourri

A pot-pourri is not a mere mixture of sachet herbs, spices and oils. It is a symphony of sweet scented rose petals and other aromas. Pot-pourri is derived from the French and means to rot. It describes the old art of preserving the precious floral scents of herbs by placing their dried petals or flower heads in jars, with salt added. "This custom," wrote Lillian M. Cronk, in *Home Garden,* "originated in ancient times when people needed sweet aromatic scents to relieve the oppressive air that accumulated in their damp, poorly ventilated and almost windowless dwellings."

The scent of herbs recall memories of summer and gardens and leisurely days. If placed in a closet or about the room with covers removed for a short time, the perfume escaping from these delightful sweet jars fills the air with a delightful fragrance. The scent pervades, not invades, a room. The jars retain their fragrance for long periods of time.

Making pot-pourris require but a scant fraction of your spare time, certainly no more than for a sachet, a sauce, or salad; nor does it demand any expensive or unusual ingredients. The air-dried petals of roses provide the base to which any of your favorites listed under *Sachets* may be added. Consider these also: anise, basil, cardomon, coriander, chamomile, hollyhock flowers, mints and phlox. For extra color, delphinium, peonies and pansies have been suggested.

To vary your mixtures, add a few drops of these essential aromatic oils which may be obtained from your druggist: bergamot, eucalyptus, sassafras, coriander, marjoram, verbena, rosemary, neroli, patchouli, lemon balm, lemon and orange.

The fixatives are the powdered or the finely ground roots of orris and sweet flag and gum benzoin, which prevent the volatile ingredients from evaporating too rapidly. My choice of fixative is orris root, which may generally be obtained from an herbalist or from some druggists. (Sweet flag is easily located in its natural habitat, quickly dried and ground, and soon made ready for use.) One ounce of the fixative (either one or a mixture of all) is needed for every quart of rose petals.

Procedure: To a quart of dried rose petals contained in an earthenware jar (we have used a cookie jar) add an ounce of the fixative and again mix. Cover and allow to so set for several weeks. You might then add a few drops of either oil of bergamot, lavender or patchouli. Repack into smaller jars. Pot-pourri makes a splendid gift.

For a moist pot-pourri alternate layers of salt and rose petals in a suitable jar and place a fairly heavy weight upon the top of the petals to hold them down. To prevent molding, stir the mixture every other day. After three weeks, remove the entire mixture, add the fixative (1 ounce to 1 quart of rose petals) and replace the petals. Add the other ingredients.

POT-POURRI I   In a covered earthen crock place a layer of rose leaves sprinkled with table salt. Continue in this manner until all your roses are used. Let them stand 5 days, stirring and turning every day.

The mixture should now appear moist. Add 3 ounces bruised allspice and 2 ounces bruised stick cinnamon. This now forms the stock. Allow it to remain a week, turning daily.

Mix 1 ounce allspice, 1 ounce cloves, 1 ounce cinnamon, 2 ounces orris root, a little ginger root sliced, 2 ounces powdered lemon or orange peel, and dried lavender flowers. Put in layers with the stock, then add a few drops of any essential oil, preferably lavender or bergamot.

This will finally shrink down about one half, in the crock.

POT-POURRI II   Select petals from full-blown, sweetest-scented roses; put to dry in dark, airy place and sprinkle with salt. Stir and turn daily for five days. Then add to each pint of dried salted petals the following: ½ tsp. ground cinnamon, ½ tsp. ground cloves, a few dried leaves of lemon verbena, rosemary, and lavender, and a little orris root powder. Stir together and set away in a sealed jar to blend and season.

Herbs for the Bath

Centuries ago, herbs were used for washing by the poor because of the prohibitive cost of soap. Many of the herbs mentioned below were popular in Elizabethan days to aromatize the warm baths. For example, chamomile "did take away weariness and ease the paines to what part of the body it be applied." This is just as true today. Equal parts of bladderwrack, marigold and nettle are "used as a cleansing invigorator." The nettle herb is used by the British in a hot bath for muscular aches. The Creek Indians used twigs of the spice bush in steam baths.

Basic herbs for the bath are balm, catnip, chamomile, hops, mints, pine, rosemary and thyme. Use any of the herbs (not spices) listed under *Sachets,* plus bladderwrack (sea-weed), meadowsweet, spice bush, and sweet flag.

Joseph E. Meyers gives these directions for using herbs in the bath. "Place dried herbs in muslin bag. Scald bag of herbs with sufficient water to well cover them, and allow to stand for at least two hours. When bath is desired pour liquid from herbs into bath water. Use bag of herbs like sponge. Do not rub the body with the bag but gently sponge. Soap must not be used. In all cases where the bath is of hot water, a cold shower or cold rub must follow. This is easiest done by wringing a towel out in cold water. Give the whole of the body a brisk rub down with it as you get out of the bath, and thoroughly dry in usual way."

In these hectic times, try relaxing in this way. Take a bath to soothe the nerves. Mix in a cheesecloth a handful each of rosemary, thyme, and mint, half a handful of lavender, one orange peel and one tablespoon dried lemon peel. Add the hot water and steep 10 minutes. Temper bath 20 minutes more.

Herbs for the Hair

Many culinary herbs are used for either setting, shampooing, tinting or dying hair and the history of their application dates back long before Cleopatra's time. The outstanding hair dye for brunettes was—and still is today—henna. It is recorded that it made dark or drab hair a brilliant auburn. It was also used on the nails of the fingers and toes. Even men used the herb for dying their beards and for coloring the manes and tails of their horses. In ancient Rome the beauticians of those days employed the expressed juice of elder berries, or a strong decoction of the fruits, as a hair dye for their more stylish patrons. In Elizabethan days, it was a common practice to massage a balding head with the ashes of southernwood mingled with old salad oil. Today, our native and culinary herbs are just as effective in tonsorial preparations as they were a hundred or a thousand years ago.

Castor oil is valuable for its emollient and healing effects in seborrhea, scalp dryness and other skin disorders. If there is a temporary condition of dandruff or excessive dryness of the scalp, warm a little oil and massage a few drops well into the scalp two to three times a day, and then shampoo. The oil, alone or mixed equally with olive oil, should be similarly applied before shampooing at all times, except, of course, when the hair is over-oily.

A good dry shampoo when a cold or time precludes a wet shampoo is made of chamomile flowers. A small handful of them are ground to a powder and vigorously rubbed into the hair, which must then be vigorously brushed. The herb is a gentle cleanser and conditioner of the scalp.

HAIR TINTS   Simple infusions of the following herbs are harmless to the hair and they add an exciting lustre or tint to dull brown hair. Chamomile flowers will bring out highlights of blonde hair. To prepare chamomile solution, mix well 2 heaping tablespoonsful of the herb in 1½ pints of hot water and simmer 20–30 minutes. Cover until cool and strain. Shampoo the hair first. Tinting is best accomplished by brushing the solution into the hair.

The use of marigold flowers will result in a blond tint, which is prepared by infusing a heaping teaspoonful of the flowers in a pint of hot water, proceeding as directed under chamomile.

In Italy and Germany today, a similar effect is obtained from the yellow mullein flowers. An old herbal says of mullein: "An infusion of the flowers was used by the Roman ladies to tinge their tresses the golden colour so much admired in Italy, where a wash, made from mullein flowers, is valued as highly restorative."

HAIR TOUCH-UP   A touch-up brown rinse for graying hair is prepared by boiling a half cupful of the dried roots of the common grape-vine or six to ten butter walnut shucks in a quart of boiling water for 10–15 minutes. Allow the decoction to cool and strain. Store in the refrigerator. Rinse the hair once a week. The bark and twigs of tag alder and black poplar and the herb agrimony also help restore the original brown.

A deeper brown is produced by a more vigorous decoction of the brown-tinting herbs. The hulls of walnuts and herb sage may be boiled for 20 minutes (2 heaping tablespoonsful to a quart of boiling water) to yield a deep, dark brown shade. Either herb may be used alone. Sage's coloring is not a dye and is easily removed by shampooing. And to produce an even darker shade, add another heaping teaspoonful of walnut and sage to the aforementioned boiling herb mixture and allow it to simmer another 10–15 minutes. Cover, allow to cool and apply like chamomile rinse. Walnut hulls, long employed by our early colonists as a dye for clothes and rugs, produce an even deeper shade of brown, depending on the number of hulls added to the simmering mixture and how long the mixture is decocted. Remove all traces of the sage or walnut rinse long before your permanent, for it may streak under the excessive heat.

HAIR CONDITIONERS   Rosemary and sage have a strengthening effect upon the scalp. A simple infusion of either herb, using a tablespoonful to a pint of water, has been found invigorating to the scalp, to quickly remove loose dandruff and to be helpful in preventing dandruff. The common yarrow and stinging nettles are equally as effective. I have often been told by users of these herbs that a brush dipped into a decoction of nettle herb and briskly massaged into the scalp, will hasten hair growth.

An herbalist of old reminds us that a decoction of wormwood

or southernwood served as an astringent wash, presumably as a hair restorative, while a mixture of the finely powdered ashes of the two herbs in olive oil was reported to "help those that have their hair falling and are bald, and restoreth where any man lacked hair."

The finely powdered charcoal of southernwood mixed into a pomade is a well known proprietary prepared by British druggists. It helps to stimulate hair growth. Because of this tonsorial purpose the herb is also referred to as the "Old Man."

An herb vinegar for the hair and scalp is composed of one ounce each of mullein leaves, rosemary and chamomile, two ounces of burdock roots and ½ ounce of sage and two quarts of cider vinegar. Soak the herbs in the vinegar for 10 days and keep the container in a warm place. To the strained liquid add an equal amount of rain or distilled water. Rub the solution well into the scalp nightly.

TINT FOR FADED OR GRAYING HAIR To a quart of boiling water, add 2 tablespoonfuls each of rosemary and chamomile and four of sage. Stir in well, cover and allow to steep gently 15–20 minutes. Shampoo the hair first and rinse thoroughly with cool water. The herbal mixture, strained, is applied as a rinse or brushed through the hair.

II

A Culinary Herbal

5

Major Herbs

ANISE

(*Pimpinella Anisum*)

Synonym: Sweet Cumin.
Part Used: Seeds, leaves.

Anise is a dainty little plant, averaging twelve to eighteen inches in height. Each of its small, slightly yellowish-white flowers appears on a long hairy stem and in the late summer or early autumn the seeds (technically fruits) appear. These are held together by their "inner face," and when ripe, separate from each other. Note, too, the ribbed mouse-shaped seed: this is nature's way of protecting the delicate cells that contain the important volatile oil.

CULTIVATION Be positive that the previously sifted soil of the seed-bed, which should be located in the most sun, consists of one-third sand, since too rich soil will yield less of the valuable anise oil.

Sow the seeds in May or when there is no danger of future cold weather. At least one hundred days of warm weather are required for a crop. Be sure that the seeds are set where they are to grow—½ to 1 inch deep, in rows at least ten to twelve inches apart. The young seedlings should not be transplanted, due to the possible damage to the mesh of rather delicate roots.

Collect the leaves any time before the appearance of the seeds.

The seeds should be collected as soon as their summits assume a grayish-green color. Until then, the seeds adhere together, and when ripe, will separate from each other.

To remove dirt, spray with cold water all seeds intended for culinary purposes, but not those intended for future cultivation.

To dry, spread out on a fine window screening, cheesecloth rack, or over newspapers placed on the attic floor. Shake seeds occasionally to insure thorough drying.

HISTORY   This is what the ancient writers said of anise:

Hippocrates recommended that anise be raised in the herbgarden. The doctor's prescription of anise as a cough remedy is today corroborated by the fact that anethol, the essential oil of anise seeds, relieves coughs.

Pliny, the Elder, believed as early as the 1st century A.D., that since "this plant imparts a youthful look to the features," one must include the leaves and seeds of this plant in seasonings and especially the seeds in all crusts of bread.

Virgil held that to prevent indigestion, one should partake of mustacae, with a warm drink, after evening meals. Mustacae was a cake spiced with anise and cumin seeds and powdered cinnamon.

Herbalist Gerard Turner wrote in his Herbal, 1551, "Anyse maketh the breath sweeter." This remedy for halitosis is made thus: "To steep or infuse for certain daies, a few Cloves, Mace, Cinnamon, and Aniseed in the distilled water of the flowers of Rosemary, being drunke at morning and evening, taketh away the stench of the mouth and maketh it very sweet."

CULINARY USES   Anise assists digestion and prevents the bad effects which sometimes follow a free use of vegetables. Thus as the ounce of prevention, include anise leaves as an ingredient (not as a garnish) in salads of vegetables and of fruits.

The seeds are used as a substitute for caraway in honey cake, cinnamon or ginger cookies; with apples—in all forms—sauce, stewed, pies, and salads, plus powdered cinnamon.

MEDICINAL USES The aromatic seeds act as a soothing carminative and children with colic and flatulence should drink, during and after meals, a cup of warm infusion of the seeds. Anise seeds help to prevent the griping of cathartics and to disguise the unpleasantness of some medicines.

Anise seeds should also be used in home-made pectoral, or cough remedies, and be combined with licorice or hollyhock roots, horehound and honey.

For a cough remedy, make a cup of hot water and steep a half teaspoonful each of aniseed, thyme and finely cut hollyhock roots in the water. When cool, stir and strain. Add 2 teaspoonfuls of honey and drink one such cupful every 1 or 2 hours.

The medicinal virtues of anise are primarily the prevention and elimination of catarrhal conditions of the alimentary and bronchial canals.

LEMON BALM
(*Melissa Officinalis*)

Synonym: Balm, Melissa.
Part Used: Leaves.

CULTIVATION Purchase in May several three- or four-week-old plants from your florist or horticulturist. Set the plants in sanded soil in a partially shaded section of your garden, because in fertile soil, balm may become rampant. Of course, plants are easily started from seeds. In the late summer, after the plant has grown to its full height of eighteen to twenty-four inches with its pear-shaped leaves and whorls of yellowish-white flowers arising from the short leaf-stems, propagate this delightfully sweet-smelling perennial by layering or plant cuttings.

Since this herb tends to become loose and spreading, the entire plant is cut in mid-summer before the flowers are in full bloom. Trim the outer foliage occasionally and dry the sprigs by suspension.

HISTORY   John Parkinson (1629) reminds us that (lemon) balm, peppermint and thyme were profitably employed in warm baths, since these herbs will "help to comfort and strengthen the nerves and sinews." As a liniment for external pains we are advised by his contemporaries to rub the affected part with a vinegar previously steeped with balm, rosemary, lavender, and peppermint.

In olden times, the medicinal virtues were well recognized by king and peasant, for if a room needed to be cleansed of stale, foul odors, lemon balm, peppermint, lavender and other herbs were strewn about the floors or placed in direct sunlight. It is quite probable that long experience in the art of using culinary herbs led cooks to deodorize and rid the kitchen of evil-smelling odors by stirring the mixture of finely crumbled herbs in a large vessel of hot water.

The names and synonyms of this herb give further evidence as to its uses. First its common name, lemon balm: lemon— because of the distinct lemony taste due to citral, one of the components of natural oil of lemon; balm, an abbreviation of balsam, the chief constituent of most aromatic oils.

A better known synonym, bee or melissa balm, is scientifically known as *Melissa officinalis*. Melissa is from the Greek, "bee"; *mel* is Latin for "honey." The flowers of this herb offer pollen to bees for the manufacture of honey which will contain the lemon flavor. Lemon balm "is profitably planted where bees are kept. The hives of Bees being rubbed with the Leaves of Bawme causeth the bees to keep together and causeth others to come with them." No doubt, balm was located "profitably" near bee hives since its leaves were used as a remedy for bee bites.

CULINARY USES   Do you use lemon juice on broiled fish? Either place an entire lemon balm shoot, six to seven inches of the leaves or sprinkle the finely ground leaves directly over fish for a few minutes while it is still in the broiling process.

As an after-dinner drink or as a substitute for tea, try a combination of mint, lemon verbena, and balm leaves.

The undried leaves, washed, are good in vegetable salads.

Of course, there's always chowder, and that calls for a bouquet of basil and balm. Ground balm is good in chopped herring.

MEDICINAL USES   Lemon balm acts as a stimulant, diaphoretic and antispasmodic, and is indicated in feverish colds and catarrhal conditions of the alimentary system. As a remedy for nervous indigestion, I highly recommend a warm tea of the leaves as an after-meal drink or nourishing substitute for tea or coffee.

SWEET BASIL
(*Ocimum Basilicum*)

Part Used: Leaves.

Sweet basil grows about one to three feet high, bush basil only six to seven inches. Its dark green inch-long leaves are dotted with oil cells and have a spicy, clove-like aroma and taste.

CULTIVATION   "Server le basilic," to sow basil, is an old French idiomatic phrase meaning "to slander." Pliny tells us that the Romans believed that the more curses cast upon the basil seeds about to be sown, the better they would grow. You will not need curses to cultivate basil; you must only be assured of warm weather. Mid-May is not too late. Sow seeds in a bed and transplant the seedlings when about three inches high.

"Forced feedings" of fertilizers and overdoses of watering will invite disaster.

Although the outer leaves may be cut for salad use whenever needed, the upper half of the entire plant is harvested when flowers begin to open, for then the aromatic oil is at its maximum strength. However, cutting the outer leaf branches often will help the plant to grow more profusely. Preserve basil leaves for winter use by pressing down in a wide-mouth pickle crock, layers of leaves and coarse salt. When needed, a small clump of the leaves is removed and shaken free of the salt.

One basil plant allowed to go to seed will offer for future planting enough of the tiny seeds for yourself and all your relatives and friends. It has been estimated that there are 23,000 seeds to one ounce weight. The seeds should be dried on newspapers indoors for at least one week.

By all means grow sweet basil indoors throughout the winter, in flower pots and in window boxes.

HISTORY   The French call basil the herb royale. *Basileus* is Greek for "a king," and therefore, royal. In the days of the English Queens Mary and Elizabeth, the tenant farmers presented potted basil plants to the ladies and lords of the land as a simple token of friendship and well-wishing.

Centuries ago during the funeral services, the floors of the home of the recently deceased, as well as the floors of the funeral parlor and the church, were strewn with a mixture of balm, peppermint and basil, which the mourners said kept the evil spirits away. We speak today of infectious bacteria, and apply disinfectants. Basil probably performed the same antiseptic role.

The germicidal action of basil depends on the strong balsamic, camphor-based aromatic oil, which also yields ozone. A species of this herb is highly venerated by the Hindus and Malays. They regard it as one of the most sacred flowers. It is cultivated near their temples and the odoriferous oil extracted for religious use.

CULINARY USES Basil, like most culinary herbs, performs a multiple service. It adds special zip to dishes of cheese or eggs or macaroni or spaghetti, onto which the finely powdered herb is sprinkled when ready to serve and in sauce. It seasons such favorite combinations as cubed cucumbers and sour cream, vegetable salad, vinegar, and meat balls. It is most famous as a mate for tomato. Add to marjoram, rosemary, savory, and thyme in a kitchen bouquet for soups and stews.

MEDICINAL USES I have noted that some people afflicted with rheumatic pain have used basil as a means of temporarily allaying their suffering. They, like so many non-rheumatics, have enjoyed the tender young leaves prepared spinach style, and warm after-meal teas of basil, catnip and peppermint. Basil serves also as a mild tonic for nervous disorders and helps to offset stomach catarrh.

BORAGE
(*Borago Officinalis*)

Part Used: Leaves, flowers.

Borage blooms throughout the summer and adds much attractiveness to an herb garden. The star-like flowers are a bright blue, and the dark green, oval leaves have a faint cucumber flavor, which is more pronounced if the plant is grown in poor unfertilized soil. Enriched soil yields a more profuse growth of foliage.

CULTIVATION Sow seeds ¼ inch deep in light, dry soil, and in a sunny location, and thin out the young seedlings at 15 inch intervals. Borage is a quick-growing plant and may be cut for use as often as every 3 or 4 weeks. Moreover, this two-foot high annual will reseed itself for many years if unmolested.

To preserve, cut the plants half way and dry by suspension in a well-ventilated room, away from the sun's direct rays. When the herbs are perfectly dry, remove the stems, finely grind the leaves and store in clean glass jars for future meals. This method is the same as dehydrating store-bought leafy vegetables as carrot and beet tops.

Don't overlook the after dinner delicacy of candied borage flowers. These are prepared quite easily by dipping them into a weak solution of irish moss or acacia, previously flavored with peppermint leaves. When nearly dry, sprinkle with sugar and allow them to dry thoroughly on waxed paper. Stored in the refrigerator, they will keep for a considerable length of time.

HISTORY   In his *Generale Historie of Plants* herbalist Gerard wrote of borage: "Those of our time do use the floures [and the leaves, of course] in sallads, to exhilarate and make the minde glad. There be also many things made of them, used for the comfort of the heart, to drive away sorrow, and increase the joye of minde . . . Syrup made of the floures of Borage comforteth the heart, purgeth melancholly and quieteth the phrenticke [frantic] person."

Over the years, borage has proven its value as a nourishing potherb and salad ingredient.

For centuries most herbalists recommended borage as a cordial for those with heart weakness; they prescribed that the flowers and leaves were to be steeped in wine, which acted as a heart-fortifying medicine. In fact, there is a popular English drink called "cool tankard" which is composed of wine, borage flowers and lemons. This recipe may have been based on a formula of borage flowers and wine which, says Pliny, the early Greeks called "Euphrosinum" for its exhilarating and inspiring effects upon the entire system.

Borage herb is densely covered with short, whitish bristly hairs and its name is derived from *burra*, Latin for "flock of wool" or thick covering of short hairs. During the 13th century, the coarse woolen cloth worn by the London poor was called "birrus" in allusion to the flannel-like roughness of the full grown borage leaves.

Plant folklore asserted that to partake of borage ensured one's courage and strengthened a faint heart: "I, Borage—Bring always courage."

CULINARY USES   As a culinary herb, the freshly cut leaves should be rinsed carefully in cold water, and may be used in the following ways:

As a substitute for spinach. It is prepared in like manner, and when cooled, sweet or preferably sour cream is added to offset the taste of a small amount of calcium oxalate, which is present also in spinach.

In all vegetable salads. First immerse the fresh leaves in wine, strain and shred. This was a favorite dish of the Crusaders before they departed for battle.

As an added ingredient in summer vegetable soups, especially beet and cucumber. Be sure to add anise or caraway seeds.

MEDICINAL USES   The medical botanists have classified borage as a diuretic, refrigerant, pectoral, demulcent, aperient, diaphoretic, and antirheumatic because of the active constituents of this herb, which are potassium nitrate and mucilage for the most part, and smaller deposits of calcium compounds, and an appreciable percentage of the essential vitamins and chlorophyll contained in all spinach-like greens.

The desired refrigerant (body cooling) and diuretic effects are due to the action of the potassium nitrate in conjunction with the mucilage. Together they help to eliminate the undesirable catarrh and undissolved deposits along the urinary channels, and prevent the formation of kidney stones. It is believed that by improving the condition of the urinary organs, the circulation of the blood stream and, indirectly, the condition of the heart, are similarly improved. A strong infusion of borage leaves with honey is often beneficial as a demulcent in bronchial catarrhal infections to facilitate expectoration.

CARAWAY
(Carum Carvi)

Synonym: Kummel.

Part Used: Seeds, roots, young leaves.

CULTIVATION   For home use, there is little difference between wild and cultivated caraway. It thrives in waste ground and clayey soil.

Since caraway is a biennial, it is the second year's growth that produces the aromatic fruits, or "seeds" as we know them. The plant has then grown to its full height of about two feet, although I have found many a wild-growing specimen approximating three feet. The small flowers bloom during June and July and terminate in erect umbels, an umbrella-shaped arrangement, and the fruits follow four to five weeks later.

Pick fruits when fully ripe. Suspend upper half of plant until dried and thrash out. Store in tightly closed containers.

Roots and leaves are obtainable in late spring or early summer (according to taste).

HISTORY   "Come, cousin Silence! We will get a pippin of last year's graffing with a dish of caraways and then to bed." Shakespeare, it appears, must have been aware of the medicinal virtues of caraway seeds when in *Henry IV* Falstaff is invited to partake of a pippin and a dish of caraways.

Herbalist Culpepper said, "Caraway confects, once only dipped in Syrup [i.e., sugar and water] and one teaspoonful of them eaten in the morning and fasting and as many after each meal, is a most admirable remedy for those that are troubled with stomach colic."

John Parkinson wrote, "The seed is much used . . . with comfits that are taken for the cold and wind in the body, as also served for the table with fruit."

As for its origin, Pliny informs us that it is an exotic plant which derives its name, Careium, from the country of old Caria, Asia Minor, where it was first grown, and that it was principally employed in those days for culinary purposes. Caraway in fruits, pastry and starchy foods as cabbage, serves as an excellent safeguard against "gassiness," another example of preventive medicine.

CULINARY USES   Caraway is used much in the same way as most members of the Umbelliferae (umbel bearing) family—anise, celery, dill and fennel.

Bakers of rye, pumpernickel or Swedish bread will invariably add a sprinkle of caraway to the dough. These seeds should be included in stew and soup of the Hungarian goulash, Russian borscht and plain cabbage soup varieties, as well as in apple sauce, cottage and cream cheese sandwiches. A judicious sprinkle of caraways over potato salad, or ½ inch inside the about-to-be baked potato, or else boiled with jacketed potatoes is delicious. Use caraway in apple sauce when prepared without powdered cinnamon, with pickled beets, and in squash and pumpkin pie.

CARAWAY   ¼ tsp. ground caraway seeds
POTATO   ½ cup sour cream
              Mix well and add to steamed or baked potatoes.
              For a dip, add a pinch of ground dill seeds.

MEDICINAL USES   Dr. Meyrick wrote in his *Family Herbal* that "the Caraway seeds bruised and made into a poultice take away black and blue marks, occasioned by falls and bruises." Today it is recognized that many a nervous condition can be traced to functional (stomach) disorders, which in turn is corrected more by proper diet than by medication. Caraway seeds act as preventive medicine by being ingested with starchy foods (cabbage, potato, etc.) and non-nourishing pastries. Caraway prevents the possibility of catarrhal formation along the alimentary system.

A warm infusion, carefully strained, is most beneficial for colic and flatulence of infants; for adults, a mixture of caraway, fennel and mint is recommended.

CHAMOMILE
(Anthemis Nobilis)

Synonym: English, Roman or Common Chamomile.
Part Used: Flowers, upper half of herb.

CULTIVATION Chamomile likes dry, sandy soil. For the purpose of cultivation, it is recommended to transplant into garden soil a set of runners, i.e., roots, being careful to pack down the sifted soil firmly on the transplanted roots, or else to tread heavily upon them by foot. Space 2½ feet apart. Chamomile does well also in rock gardens. Collect when in full bloom.

HISTORY It is important to distinguish between the principal chamomiles. False chamomile is *Anthemis cotula,* better known as mayweed, dog or fetid chamomile, which is often found as an adulterant in the "wild" species, and which was as Gerard put it, "a ranke and naughtie smell. The whole plante stinketh and giveth a ranke smell." Yet, this species has its place in medicine as a diaphoretic in colds and rheumatism.

However, confusion persists as to the true and wild species. The former, *Anthemis nobilis,* is best known as Roman chamomile and may be described as a low growing (6–8″ high) perennial, with few solitary scaly flower heads, its yellow fading to buff. The wild or German chamomile, which has almost completely supplanted the former in medicine today, attains a growing height of 6–18″. Its ovoid flower heads are hollow rather than conical, and made up of white and yellow florets. This annual is easily grown from seed.

The genus name, *Matricaria,* is derived from the Latin word, *matrix,* and alludes to remedies of the uterus. Chamomile is derived from the Greek *kamai,* "ground," and *melon,* "apple," and refers to the distinct apple scent of this plant.

The wine-growers of Spain use chamomile flowers to flavor their light sherry wine, called manzanilla, which is Spanish for chamomile. Our domestic vermouth is now being flavored by these flowers, although this process is still in the experimental stage.

The folklore of chamomile contains much more that is fancied, less that is real. It was supposedly "very good against the biting of Serpents and all other venomous beasts, because its creeping stems resembled a wriggling serpent." It is quite doubtful whether the present day gardener would consider chamomile "the plant's physician," but years back it was believed to keep a garden healthy, especially strengthening weak plants when placed in their midst.

On the other hand, while some may ridicule the 17th century herbalist Turner's recommendation of chamomile for diseases of the eye, because "it hath flowers wonderfully shynynge yellow and resemblynge the appell of an eye," there are many pharmacists today who still dispense chamomile flowers by prescription request of modern physicians.

ECONOMIC USES Not only are chamomile flowers used to flavor domestic or foreign wines, they are also used by most cosmetologists as a wash for blonde or light hair, to tone and accentuate the natural color of the hair. In the perfume industry, the oil also finds a use as a blend in some of the oriental compounds, often in combination with patchouli, lavender and oak moss.

MEDICINAL USES This herb proves beneficial in most gastro-intestinal disorders, acting as a carminative, nerve sedative, and aromatic bitter; and its tonic properties should be employed in general debility or poor digestion and during convalescence. In the latter case, dried orange peel may be mixed in.

Equal parts of chamomile, tag alder bark and elder flowers are used today in cases involving "high blood pressure." Cupful of warm infusion three times a day.

As an after dinner drink, or as a tea substitute, one part each of chamomile and spearmint makes a most desirous herb tea, or tisane, for any who cannot tolerate either pekoe tea or coffee. In fact, as one recent commentator has said, "The French, who are perhaps the greatest connoisseurs and certainly the greatest users of these aromatic beverages, include chamomile as one of the six most favored herbs. These tisanes play an important part in French daily life, as well as constituting the first cure for ailments not serious enough to require the services of a doctor."

CHIVES
(Allium Schoenoprasum)

Part Used: Green stems.

Members of the chives group include onion, garlic, wild leek and shallot, and are related to the orchids, asparagus, and Easter and tiger lilies.

CULTIVATION Chives grow about 6 to 10 inches tall, blossoming in June or July. The flower petals are usually pale purple, dissolving into a rose color. If you want to make use of the chives as salad greens or in croquettes or in other ways later described, cut the plants close to the ground. This may be done four or five times during the growing period. Remember that the bulbs of the chive plants may be easily separated from one another and each replanted. As a garden plant chives make a most desirable and balanced edging for other herbs, and may be also grown in partial shade.

HISTORY Like the related onion and garlic, chives were employed in the more backward European countries to protect one against the Evil Eye and all diseases in general. In fact, besides being used by Romany Gypsies in their fortune-forecasts, the chive family was considered to be a "magnet of the plague." Not only would a sufferer of consumption or influenza drink hot infusions of onions or chives, he deemed it imperative that a clump of chives be suspended from the center of the sick room and from—in most cases—a bedpost within reach as well. This practice, so guaranteed the fortunetellers, was a "sure" means of drawing to the chives "maladies that would otherwise fall on the inmates."

CULINARY USES   The possibilities of herb seasoning, it has been said, can hardly be overestimated, and more so in summer when appetites lag; although it is equally profitable to have one window box contain chives throughout both summer and winter. Finely chopped, they should be included in spinach or beet soup, to which diced cucumbers have been added, in all fresh salads and in cheese omelettes. Add chives to soup and omelettes only when served. They add a new sparkle to sandwiches of cream cheese and peanut butter; and to boiled potatoes in which they are mashed. Especially adapted for those who cannot tolerate onions or garlic without visions of dyspepsia, or at least of disturbing a tender digestion, have a favorite dish, say of croquettes of fish or chicken, benefited by the judicial addition of chopped chives, seasoned with marjoram or thyme.

In fact, chives will season almost everything from soup to nutted cheese, except desserts and pastries. Chive mayonnaise is prepared by incorporating thoroughly the bulbs in the mayonnaise directly before serving. Chive vinegar and oil are obtained by several days' steeping in white vinegar or warmed salad oil. Always eat chives raw, uncooked.

Here's a cheese appetizer or hors d'oeuvres quickly prepared: Mix together a half teaspoonful each of scallions or chives and sage finely granulated and incorporate with ½ cup of cream cheese. Spread on toasted fingers or crackers.

MEDICINAL USES   Chives were employed, either alone or in combination with the more pungent onion and garlic, as a medicinal remedy for the "nerves," bronchial disorders and especially for blood diseases. The inclusion of uncooked chives in one's meals provides health sustaining vitamins and minerals, vitamin C and to a lesser degree, vitamins A, B and G, sulfur and iron. It is this sulfur component which is somewhat similar to garlic's, being the active bactericidal agent. Crotonaldehyde fortifies the nasal and respiratory areas against diseases. Moreover, the members of the chive family stimulate the saliva and digestive juices while at the same time performing the duties of intestinal antiseptic. A syrup of chives, or better of onion or garlic, serves well as a cold-cough remedy especially useful in croup or spasms of asthma. Moreover, the old onion remedy for infected burns and sores has truly won deserving merit. It has been recently discovered that freshly macerated onions contain volatile substances, called phytoncides, killers of plant bacteria, which will quickly kill protozoa and bacteria.

DILL
(Anethum Graveolens)

Part Used: Ripe fruits (seeds). Whole plant.

HISTORY   Dill was one of the plants used by the magicians and the superstitious during the Middle Ages to cast spells against witchcraft, these lines being twice chanted:

> "There with her Vervain and her Dill,
> That hindreth Witches of their will"

CULTIVATION   It is of very easy culture. Sow the seeds in drills 10 inches apart in April and every 6 weeks for a plentiful supply.

Once the seedlings are thinned out, about 8 inches apart, be sure to mat the area with straw or leaf refuse. Dill is a self-sower.

CULINARY USES   Ends of tips of the feathery foliage of dill may be clipped when the plant has grown about 3 feet high and used freshly ground in tomato soup, or in 6–8 inch lengths sprinkled over boiled meats and fish. The cut leaves are especially good in sandwiches of cream cheese and cottage cheese dishes. Let the seeds stand for 1 or 2 days in cottage or cream cheese before serving. The taste of dill resembles fennel but is more pungent.

For pickled cucumbers, place layer of ripe dill plant on bottom of open crock, then cucumbers. Repeat until full. Mix with salt and add 2 oz. alum to a gallon of water. Fit wooden boards over mixture and over all, place a heavy stone to keep the mixture well compacted.

To store dill plant for the winter pack down the young stems and leaves between layers of salt in a crock, and they will remain green and quite flavorsome throughout the winter season. The entire herb may also be stored in the attic by suspension drying.

Fry fillet of whiting, butter fish or flounder in the usual way, adding a clove of garlic to the fat. When the fish is fried, remove it to a hot platter and sprinkle generously with finely chopped dill. Cover and let steam for several minutes before serving. Fish seasoned in this way is delicious cold.

Chopped dill is good added to the warm sauce served with boiled meat or cauliflower.

MEDICINAL USES   Nicholas Culpepper, an herbal authority of the 1600's, has stated that "The seed is of more use than the leaves, and more effective to digest raw and viscous humors, and is in medicines that serve to expel wind and pains proceeding therefrom." Today, several hundred years after Culpepper's time, dill seeds (fruits) are used for the same medicinal purposes, only now the terms used are more impressive—"aromatic" and "carminative." Dill water was a favorite "grandmother's" remedy for nausea and stomach distress. However, for colic and flatulence of infants and the elderly, a mixture of equal amounts of dill, anise and fennel in warm infusion is recommended.

Hence, the derivation of the name "dill," which is said to have been derived from an old word, dilla—to lull, alluding to the soothing carminative properties of the plant. For this reason, dill seeds should be combined with other stomachic preparations, laxatives especially.

FENNEL
(*Foeniculum Vulgare*)

Part Used: Ripe fruit, seeds.

CULTIVATION   The herb may easily be grown from seed, either in late spring or early fall, by sowing seed directly into drills not more than ½ inch deep and 2 feet apart and covered lightly. Care must be taken to thin out the seedlings at least 15-18 inches apart. The New England gardener treats this herb as an annual.

Fennel being a perennial, its fruits mature and are collected during the summer of the second year's growth when they assume a greenish-gray color.

HISTORY   The fruits and edible succulent shoots of fennel were utilized by the ancient Romans and Greeks, and by the people before them. This herb was not only highly recommended by the great Greek physician Hippocrates, but considered by Pliny to possess at least two-score remedies, some of which are herein discussed.

Fennel's slenderizing effects have been often commented upon. Herbalist William Coles stated, in *Nature's Garden*: "Both the seeds, leaves and root of our Garden Fennel are much used in drinks and broths for those that are grown fat, to abate their unwieldiness and cause them to grow more gaunt and lank."

Furthermore, it is quite probable that the ancient Greeks knew of this property for they called it *marathon,* derived from *maraino,* "to grow thin."

No herb garden should be considered complete without at least 3–4 fennel plants which make good use of neglected clayey soil.

This hardy perennial grows some 2 to 4 feet high and has characteristics peculiar to itself. The carrot-like leaves spread out like the ends of the nervous system of the human body, and the rather stout stems are cylindrical, bright green and very smooth, seemingly recently polished. The small golden flowers which bloom in July and August are so arranged in what the botanist calls an "umbel" that at first glance one is sharply reminded of miniature umbrellas.

CULINARY USES Fennel has generally been associated with fish. The rather indigestible oil of that food is counter-balanced by the carminative aromatic properties of the herb. As Culpepper aptly put it, "One good old custom is not yet left off, viz., to boil Fennel with fish, for it consumes the phlegmatic humours which fish most plentifully afford and annoy the body with, though few that use it know wherefore they do it."

The leaves and stalks may be included in vegetable salads, with broiled mackerel or croquetted salmon. The stalks, peeled, may be eaten either as celery or cooked asparagus-fashion. Use the dried leaves finely ground in soup and vinegars.

MEDICINAL USES The conservative U.S. Dispensatory has said, "Fennel seed is one of our most grateful aromatics . . . corrigent of other less pleasant medicines, particularly Senna and Rhubarb. In infants, the infusion is frequently employed as an enema of the expulsion of flatus . . . Fennel water is a pleasant vehicle with a flavor suggestion of Anise water." Fennel seeds (fruits) can be used as a stimulant and carminative.

Fennel has been used as an eye-wash and the following formula may be used:

> Fennel
> Chamomile
> Eyebright
> Hot boiled water, one cupful
> Directions: Steep ⅛ teaspoonful of each herb in the water until it is cool. Stir, strain and filter carefully. Wash eye with eye-cup every 3-4 hours as required.

A most effective flea powder may be prepared by mixing one part of powdered fennel and ten parts of pyrethrum (insect flowers).

SWEET FENNEL
(*Foeniculum Dulce*)

Synonym: Finnochio, Florence Fennel, Anise (misnomer).
Part Used: Fresh leaves and stalks.

This variety has borne the misnomer "anise" because of its anise-licorice-like taste, and is preferred by Italian chefs for salads and soups. A biennial, it reaches a full-grown height of two feet and should be cultivated in rich soil, as with celery. The seeds may be gathered during the summer of the second year.

Use finnochio, the first year's growth, as a celery substitute. The stalks and swollen bases should be included in all mixed salads, vegetable, fruit, chicken or fish. Use the fresh foliage as a sprinkle over soups and salads.

If one need cook any portion of finnochio, do not overcook, never boil—but steam only two or three minutes.

MARJORAM
(*Origanum Marjoram*)

Synonym: Sweet Marjoram. Pot or Dwarf Marjoram.
Part Used: Upper half of herb, especially the leaves.

CULTIVATION In the north, marjoram is usually considered an annual and a profuse crop may be had utilizing a sunny spot where the soil is unusually sandy. In the autumn, immediately after the last cutting of marjoram, a heavy mulch of the green leaves of the native dandelion, burdock and grass cuttings, laden down with stones, will in most cases insure against winter-kill.

There are three methods of cultivation:

1. By seed: The quite small seeds should be mixed with sifted sand and soil and then sown in flats. This should be done in the spring, or, they may be started by your florist or horticulturist.

Germination is very slow and may be hastened by placing wet burlap over newly sown seeds. The diminutive seedlings may tease you with their snail-paced growth, but do not try to hurry them by extra fertilizer. The 2–3 inch seedlings are then potted for indoors or placed outdoors after all danger of frost has passed. Don't crowd the plants; do space about 2 feet apart.

2. Root cuttings: These should be potted in early spring and transplanted to the garden plot in mid-June.

3. Layering: Use hardy stems only of mature plants.

Be sure to cut the leaf tops before full bloom of the flowers, at least three times during the growing season. In the fall, as you prepare to mulch your garden herbs, pot one or two marjoram plants for your window garden, so that you may have a continual supply of the herb. Be sure, however, to place in, or near, the direct sunlight.

HISTORY With many herb sachets or usual mixture of herbs there is usually associated some bit of folklore. Upon retiring, the young debutantes of years ago would anoint themselves on St. Luke's day with a mixture, or sachet, of marigold, thyme, and marjoram, and repeat the following lines three times in the hope that their dreams of a future husband would be fulfilled: "St. Luke, St. Luke, be kind to me, In dreams, let me my true love see."

Among the early Greeks and Romans, marjoram was grown on graves to perpetuate the peace of the departed, while at marriage ceremonies sprigs of marjoram were often used to crown the happy couple.

There is a Greek myth of a certain young man who was employed by Cinyras, King of Cyprus. As one authority writes, "One day this young man was carrying a vase of perfume which he dropped. So great was his humiliation that he became unconscious, and the gods changed him into the sweet herb Marjoram."

CULINARY USES   Use for seasoning as often as possible.

Use freshly collected leaves in summer sandwiches of chicken or cheese. The fresh herb is a must in all vegetable salads. Try it with asparagus, new peas or with spinach.

To prepare "Hollywood Chicken Sandwiches": A half teaspoonful finely ground or powdered marjoram mixed with 2 tablespoonfuls salad dressing and blended with one cup of minced cooked chicken and ¼ cup finely chopped toasted almonds will make about 5 sandwiches.

Either alone or with summer savory and thyme, it adds a pleasing flavor to gravy, stuffings, soups and stews. Sprinkle lightly over all meats and fish; goes very well with hamburger and frankfurters as evidenced by its use by most commercial meat packers.

Be sure to include any extra aromatic leaf stems of the marjoram plant in your fragrant pot-pourri and sachets. The distilled volatile oil has been employed to scent toilet articles and soaps.

The characteristic spicy flavor of marjoram is good in herb vinegar: about 3 ounces of the fresh leaves collected before flowering—later in the fall use the stems and trimmings—to a pint of cider vinegar. Let stand 2 weeks before straining. Use as indicated above.

MEDICINAL USES   The camphoraceous principle contained·in the leaf oil causes marjoram to be employed as a medicinal: to relieve a simple headache or nervousness by drinking a warm infusion of marjoram, catnip and peppermint, 1 part each, and of sage ½ part.

To hasten the eruption in measles, and act to overcome the fever, a hot tea of equal parts of catnip and marjoram is occasionally employed in folk-practice. Add a pinch of saffron.

Gerard informs us that he and his herbalist contemporaries signified sweet marjoram as a "remedy against cold diseases of the brain and head [dizziness or headache] . . . It easeth the toothache being chewed in the mouth . . . The leaves boiled in water, and the decoction drunke easeth such as are given to over-much sighing . . . The leaves dried and mingled with honey put away black and blew markes after stripes and bruises, being applied thereto."

PARSLEY
(*Petroselinum Crispum*)

Part Used: Herb.

CULTIVATION   The "Prince of Biennial Herbs" will flourish no matter where, no matter what soil. Choose a partially shaded section in odd corners of the flower garden and ordinary, well-worked, and even better, moist soil. Sow the seeds in drills or distribute them thinly in "poor" soil. They may also be cultivated as an edging or between rows of lettuce or other small-sized crops. Successive plantings take place in the first week of April (if soil can be readied), mid-May and late July or early August, thus presenting an almost constant supply of the worthy plant. Transplant the one to two inch seedlings 8 inches apart and water well in dry weather.

CULINARY USES   Parsley should always be eaten uncooked—by itself, in salads, on just about any kind of food.

MEDICINAL USES   If your system lacks Vitamin A, think twice before wasting parsley as a garnish or a seasoning for soup or not eating it at all. It is one of the richest food sources of vitamins and minerals. In comparison to the Vitamin A content of carrots (5,500 units), parsley offers at least 40,000 units per ounce, which also, is about four times that of spinach. Moreover, it contains almost as much Vitamin C as an orange and an appreciable quantity of Vitamin B factors, thiamin, riboflavin and niacin.

Parsley contains these four vital minerals: calcium, copper, iron and manganese—the better to strengthen and "purify" your blood stream.

Both parsley leaves and seeds (ripe fruits) possess medicinal virtues. The leaves are of great benefit as a diuretic, when the indications are stones and congestion in the kidneys, dropsy, and the like. The seeds are of special service in amenorrhea and dysmenorrhea.

Eat a handful of parsley to mask the tale-telling odors of liquors, onion and garlic.

ROSEMARY
(*Rosemarinus Officinale*)

Synonym: Incensier (French).
Part Used: Upper half of herb.

CULTIVATION   Start the plants from seeds and stem cuttings. In the northern states, the herb winterkills easily and so must be treated as an annual. One plant is sufficient for the average household's needs.

HISTORY   The pungent aroma of rosemary's aromatic oil was familiar to the Europeans of the past few centuries, who made profitable use of its disinfecting and germicidal properties by strewing the ground herb upon the floors of churches and meeting places, after weddings and funerals. Rosemary was employed by the superstitious of Italy and Spain during the Dark Ages—

"to ward off the evil spirits." It was sprinkled in places where it was imagined the evil spirits lurked ready to spread disease and destruction.

Until very recently, a mixture of rosemary and juniper berries was the only method used in many of the French hospitals, to cleanse the sick-rooms of foul odors and to prevent the spreading of contagious infections. The French call it the "Incensier Method." Take a handful each of juniper and rosemary; crush and stir them well in a pan containing about a quart of hot water, which is kept over a radiator, or stove, during the winter; or in the summer, herb sprigs may be stationed at the window, in the direct path of the sun rays. Before long, the steaming herb vapors containing minute quantities of rosemary's volatile oil— and juniper's—will provide antiseptic benefits throughout the room and the air will be soon cleansed of foul odors.

CULINARY USES   Rosemary is strongly flavored, and it must be used sparingly at all times. A meagre sprinkle of this herb will suffice to enhance the main flavor of lamb or veal roasts, and too, of meat stews and vegetable soups.

One restaurateur has suggested to me that a generous pinch of thyme and a scant one of rosemary can be added to calf's liver, or combined with marjoram, for eggplant and zucchini. He uses rosemary with spaghetti.

With fried potatoes, sprinkle a bit of rosemary and summer savory into the frying fat.

The fresh leaves may also be chopped up with parsley and mixed with cheese (cottage or cream) for sandwich fillings, and as with other culinaries may be added to vegetable plates, hot or cold.

Prepare your own herb jelly or jam and sauce that is to be served with the usual protein foods.

MEDICINAL USES   We are told by the herbalists of former days that "the distilled water of the flowers of Rosemary taketh the stench [of the mouth] away." This solution helps to counteract "halitosis."

Though it is not usually included in the category of medicinal herbs, rosemary may be added to herb mixtures that are intended to relieve nervous headaches (see under marjoram), colic in adults and systematic colds. It may also be mixed with ground leaves of mullein and coltsfoot and employed in cases of asthma, either as an herb tea or as a syrup.

OTHER.USES   To prepare a desirable post-shampoo rinse for all shades of hair: Infuse in a pint of water for a day one ounce of rosemary and sage leaves, strain, and then add one teaspoonful of powdered borax. This preparation should be employed as "hair tonic" for loose dandruff or itchy scalp.

As a valuable moth preventive and potpourri, use with lavender flowers and ground lemon peel.

Many bee-keepers of California have taken to the cultivation of rosemary so that its distinctive flavor may be imparted to the honey.

Violin makers finish their products with a special varnish of amber and oils of linseed, turpentine and rosemary.

SAGE
(*Salvia Officinalis*)

Synonym: Garden Sage.
Part Used: Leaves.

I cannot imagine any vegetable garden without at least 4 or 5 sage plants. This herb is a hardy, healthy one that produces an abundance of quickly germinating seeds.

CULTIVATION   Sage is a low growing perennial of maximum height 2 to 2½ feet, which will thrive nearly as well in part-shade as in open sun. Our 9-foot-square bed of sage near the apple mint has done quite well under the huge maple tree. Cuttings may be taken during mid-summer and again in the fall; the annual pruning should be done in July.

Propagation is best by cuttings and root divisions of the second year plants. During the rainy season insert the cuttings in the bed where they are to grow and surround with leaf mulch. Seeds are planted in a box-tray or the coldframe, and the young plants transplanted in April and spaced about a foot apart. To be protected against winter-kill, the plants must be cut down to 4 to 6 inches of the ground and mulched with oak leaves, which in turn is covered with a few stones. This is best done after an early frost.

HISTORY   Sage was aptly named by the ancients. Its botanical name, *Salvia,* is derived from Latin *salvere,* to save or to heal, as is our word salve, or ointment.

Sage has been associated with longevity, as illustrated by these two proverbs:

> How can a man die who has Sage in his garden?
> —Arabian.

> He that would live for aye
> Must eat Sage in May.
> —Old English.

The herbalist recommends that one drink warm teas of sage two or three times a day during the few weeks of spring (from March 15 to the third or fourth week of May and during every month of the calendar). This herb infusion (tisane) is a good old "spring tonic," and will do wonders to tone up the system and get rid of that leftover winter lethargy. One may live "for aye," or at least to a fairly ripe old age.

Gerard said: "Sage is singular good for the head and braine; it quickenth the senses and memory, strengthens the sinews, restoreth health to those that have the palsie, takes away shaking or trembling of the members, and being put up into the nosthrils, it draweth their flegme out of the head."

Herbalist Culpepper was more specific and declared that the herb, among its many uses, is "good for diseases of the liver and to make blood. A decoction of the leaves and branches of Sage made and drunk, saith Dioscorides, provokes urine and causeth hair to become black. It stayeth the bleeding of wounds and cleaneth ulcers and sores . . . It is profitable for all pains in the head coming of cold rheumatic humors, as well as for all pains in the joints, whether inwardly or outwardly. The juice of Sage in warm water cureth hoarseness and cough. Pliny saith it cureth stinging and biting serpents. Sage is of excellent use to help the memory, warming and quickening the senses. The juice of Sage drunk with vinegar hath been of use in the time of the plague at all times. Gargles are made with Sage, Rosemary, Honeysuckles and Plantains, boiled in wine or water with some honey or alum put thereto, to wash sore mouths and throats, as need requireth."

Here is a basic recipe for poultry stuffing and kitchen bouquet:

One part each of sage, marjoram, thyme, summer savory. Use this combination also for soup and stews.

Here is a sage and onion sauce:

Chop very fine 1 oz. of onion and ½ oz. green sage leaves and put them into a stew-pan with 4 teaspoonfuls of water, simmer gently for 10 minutes, then put in a teaspoonful of pepper and salt substitute, plus 1 oz. of fine bread crumbs; mix well together; then pour into it a quarter of a pint of broth or gravy or melted butter, stir well together and simmer it a few minutes longer. For roast pork, poultry, geese or ducks, or green peas.

However, to use sage, use a bit of discretion. Beginners in herb cookery should include only half of the amount called for in any recipe. Let the taste of sage "grow" on you, to add a new sparkle to your culinary art.

When having cheese, broiled meats, stewed tomatoes or string beans, a judicious sprinkle of finely ground sage leaves will provide proper seasoning.

MEDICINAL USES   Sage herb provides a most desirable substitute for tea or coffee. For mealtime drinks, use about ½ teaspoonful of sage either alone or with equal portions of mint and ground lemon peel. A little hot vinegar added to this warm compound tea provides a good application for sprains and bruises. Apply as a compress as warm as can be tolerated to the affected parts.

The Chinese prized quite highly and even preferred sage to their own tea. This herb was recognized as a stimulating tonic when sipped in the manner of a mealtime beverage. It is recorded that in trading with the early Dutch traders, they were willing to accept one pound of sage for three of their own pekoe.

Many are the uses of this rather prodigious herb and much has been written of its many and valued medicinal actions over the centuries.

Medicinal Sage Recipes

GARGLE AND CANKER WASH	Sage Sumac berries Gold Thread One ounce of each. Boil sumac and gold thread in 1½ pints of hot water for a half hour, add sage and simmer another ½ hour. This solution is equally effective as a dressing application to scratches or wounds.
GENERAL NERVE TONIC	Catnip 4 parts Scullcap 4 parts Sage 2 parts Chamomile 4 parts Valerian 2 parts Add a heaping teaspoonful to a cup of hot water and cover half an hour. Stir, strain and drink a wine glassful every 2 or 3 hours, if condition is serious. Otherwise, drink a cupful four times a day.
GENERAL STOMACHIC FOR NERVOUS STOMACH OR DYSPEPSIA	Sage 1 part Mint 2 parts Catnip 2 parts Linden 2 parts Teaspoonful to a cup of hot water and cover 20 minutes. Stir, strain and drink ½ such cupful as necessary or ½ hour before and after meals.
DIAPHORETIC SWEATING AGENT	Use ingredients of the stomachic above and add 2 parts each of boneset and yarrow and prepare

IN SYSTEMATIC
COLDS
as before. Cover for 10 minutes only and drink one cupful every hour or sooner, until desired effects result. This formula will provide more than an ounce of prevention against possible winter colds if taken morning and night.

SUMMER SAVORY
(*Satureia Hortensis*)

Synonym: Savory.
Part Used: Leaves. Flowering tops.

Of the 14 species of savory, only two are generally accepted by the herb user or gourmet: summer savory, the annual; and winter savory, the perennial. The latter possesses a more peppery flavor than that of the summer, but is seldom used when the summer variety is available. The summer variety is the favorite and by far much more often employed, although the two are interchangeable in usual recipes—stews, soups, meat and fish dishes.

Fully grown, it acquires an average height of 12–15 inches. Its dainty pink to lilac flowers are borne on erect slender stems. The half-inch leaves will appear to be bunched together on the upper half of the plant.

Many centuries ago the leaves of this herb were rubbed on fresh insect bites and bee stings, and today, for that same reason, savory is generally grown about beehives—and, to add a distinctive flavor to the honey.

CULTIVATION Upon your patience will depend the results of your cultivating summer savory. Its seeds are very slow to germinate. The soil should be of the ordinary garden variety, unfertilized and undiluted with sand. Sow the seeds ⅛ inch deep, every sixth inch and space the rows 15 inches apart. When 6–8 inches high the young seedlings require loose open growth without interference.

The foot high plants should be topped or cut when the flowers first appear, and cut again ten weeks later, around August 20–30th. After all the leaves have been removed, the remaining herb stalks should not be discarded as worthless. Save these woody portions. These stems, fresh or dried, should be ground up coarsely and incorporated into an herb vinegar; or may be mixed with usually discarded dried tangerine or lemon peels, to prepare a kitchen bouquet.

CULINARY USES Continental Europeans have long associated this herb with "beanes and pease," just as we consider basil a must with tomato and fennel with fish. For that reason, savory is referred to by chefs of European descent as Bohnenkraut. This word is derived from two German words—*Bohne* meaning bean and *Kraut*, herb. Therefore, savory is the herb for baked or string beans and peas and all starchy vegetables.

In considering the manifold uses of savory, one should remember that it is considered by all concerned a "good mixer" and will often be seen in the company of marjoram and thyme.

Use with marjoram and thyme in poultry stuffing. Flavor may be added to duck stuffing by mixing ½ teaspoonful of savory to each heaping tablespoonful of combined rinds, fresh or dried, of lemon, orange and tangerine. The mixture should be allowed to "set" in a cup of warm burgundy wine for one hour before incorporating the other finely ground ingredients.

Alone or with marjoram and thyme, it should be added to dressings other than mayonnaise, to gravies and sauces.

HISTORY Certain writers urge us to remember well the derivation and meaning of the Latin names of savory and then, say they, will one better appreciate its properties and uses . . . *Satureia* (or *Satureja*) may be derived from *satyr* which, according to mythology, was a "sylvan demigod, part man and part god, or part he-goat, who was the common attendant on Bacchus and characterized by riotous merriment and lasciviousness." However, a more pertinent interpretation of the derivation of savory is "having savor or relish, pleasing to the organs of the taste and smell, appetizing and palatable."

Hortensis is taken from the Latin word, *hortus*, garden, and means "fit or belonging to a garden."

Savory is a member of the mint family, and is often called European Mint.

MEDICINAL USES   A warm infusion of the leaves (see formula which follows) will often correct a severe case of flatulence or wind colic, for which savory is considered by some writers a specific remedy. When drunk warm, this infusion is beneficial in feverish colds. Savory adds its aromatic and taste-disguising qualities to a typical combination of such bitterish herbs as yarrow and boneset, with the result that this worthy trio becomes more acceptable as an excellent "cold breaker" to the neophyte user of herb mixtures.

The savory infusion drunk cold—either alone or with the yarrow and boneset, acts as a gentle and stimulating tonic after a siege of a cold or cough, or both.

The volatile oil of summer savory has been used to relieve the pain of toothache and applied to the tooth cavities in manner similar to oil of cloves. However, whenever there is indicated an inflammation of the gums or the tooth area, the following mixture may be employed as a poultice: finely ground hops—1 part, ground sassafras bark—2 parts, finely ground sweet savory—1 part. Of this mixture, a half teaspoonful contained in muslin cloth, is steeped in hot water and applied to the affected area. Apply every half hour for best results.

ANTI-COLIC   Summer Savory
                    Catnip
                    Mint
                    Chamomile
                       Directions: Mix equal parts of each and stir a
                    teaspoonful in a cup of hot water and cover 10-15

minutes. Stir, strain and drink one cupful every
2-3 hours as needed.

On coarse, fatty or oily foods, savory tends to prevent a possible
dangerous catarrhal condition in the intestines known as colitis.
Such beneficial action is due principally to the carvacrol constituent of the volatile oil. Marjoram, thyme, and savory all contain a greater percentage of the substance known as carvacrol
than of the other active ingredients.

WINTER SAVORY
(*Satureja Montana*)

Part Used: Leaves. Flowering tops.

This perennial is much more woody than the summer variety
and 6 or 7 plants will add much to an herb garden. The plant
grows to a height of 16 inches.

Cultivation is usually from seed and when the seedlings are
4 inches high, set about 18 inches apart. It is also propagated by
April cuttings of young shoots or division of the roots.

Winter savory prefers soil that is poor and stony.

Collect the leaves when flowers begin to bloom, and use as
with summer savory or thyme, especially in poultry stuffing or
with onion and parsley.

GARDEN THYME
(*Thymus Vulgaris*)
WILD CREEPING THYME
(*Thymus Serepyllum*)

Part Used: Leaves. Flowering tops.

CULTIVATION   Creeping thyme is best suited as a ground cover
and will generally thrive in dry, "poor" areas. It will do equally
as well between damp bricks or flagstones, in rock gardens and

along walks for ornamental purposes. The shrubby garden variety will need much more room and require garden or field space.

The soil conditions for thyme culture are simple. It prefers stony, light and well drained soil. If the soil is garden rich, it should be thinned out with ordinary road sand.

Thyme may be propagated from seed or plant divisions. The seed may be started in early spring indoors or under glass in an outdoor bed, and transplanted when seedlings are three inches high. Seeds can be sown in late spring in rows three feet apart and covered lightly. It has been estimated that there are more than 150,000 seeds per ounce weight.

Cuttings of the crown system will root easily if taken in July just before the plant blooms, and care must be taken to slip a piece of the plant with roots attached. Best rooting conditions are under glass and in sand. Transplantings of seedlings or cuttings should be watered well.

New plants should be started from seed every three or four years if the old plants have become too woody to produce enough of the small delicate leaves to make the effort worthwhile; nor will older plants produce a good grade of tender stems for cutting.

Thyme leaves may be harvested before flowering or when flower buds are forming, and dried indoors away from the direct sunlight which tends to fade the leaves. Three cuttings may be afforded, the last in October.

When seed is desired, spread a cloth or sheets of paper beneath the plant and allow the seed to drop on them as it ripens. Twice daily (12 and 4 P.M.) plants should be gently jarred to make the ripe seeds fall into the sheets.

CULINARY USES   Use in fish and clam chowder, tomato and onion soups; gumbo or thick vegetable soups, with all meats, in all stuffing and fricassee, in all sauces. Try it with your next egg or cheese omelctte. With starchy vegetables, and beets and carrots.

Equal portions of summer savory, marjoram and thyme for cottage or cream cheese, plain or hors d'oeuvres, or sandwiches. Herb jelly with the usual protein dishes (cheese, fish or meat). Herb vinegar to be mixed with mayonnaise or other dressing.

MEDICINAL USES   The label on a bottle of Pertussin says that it is composed of a "Saccharated extract of Thyme," which is mixed with sugar and water to form this syrup. It is of benefit in whooping and bronchial cough—and a reasonable facsimile can be made right in your own kitchen merely by steeping or simmering wild thyme herb in warm water, the "standard" remedy for centuries. A strong infusion of thyme, drunk in the manner of tea, is effectual remedy for headaches, giddiness and other disorders of that kind; and it is a certain remedy for that troublesome complaint, the nightmare.

No less than one of America's foremost pharmacognacists, Professor Heber W. Youngken, had for nearly two decades been teaching the students at the Massachusetts College of Pharmacy that the medicinal properties of garden thyme (*T. Vulgaris*) are antispasmodic, carminative and stimulant; of wild thyme (*T. Serepyllum*), "antispasmodic in the treatment of whooping cough and dry nervous asthma, severe spasms with little sputum, and other respiratory inflammation."

Include thyme with rosemary as a disinfectant for a sick-room. It contains thymol and carvacrol. The volatile oil which is distilled from the flowering plant is an active ingredient in two of the druggist's items—Antiseptic Solution and Compound Ephedrine Spray. Thymol, Professor Youngken says, has been employed as an "anthelmintic for hook worms, as an antiseptic and deodorant in mouth washes and gargles," and occasionally as an intestinal antiseptic.

Perhaps the derivation of thyme will help to emphasize the usage of the herb. It is taken from the Latin, *fumus,* meaning to smoke, fume, steam, and from the Greek word *thymiana* (sacrifice) suggesting an herb used as incense "to perfume or disinfect the temples." The oil of thyme, according to the U.S. Dispensatory, is "powerfully germicidal."

"BLOOD CLEANSER" FORMULA

Thyme Leaves
Watercress Leaves
Blueberry Leaves
Sassafras Bark

Directions: Mix equal parts of the ingredients. Steep a teaspoonful of the mixture in a cup of hot water, and let stand until cool, covered with a saucer. Stir, strain and drink one such cupful 4 times a day.

6

Minor Herbs

BURNET
(*Sanguisorba Minor*)

Synonym: Salad Burnet.
Part Used: The fresh leaves.

Burnet possesses a tender cucumber flavor which is lost to a marked degree upon drying.

It is easily cultivated from seed, preferably as a perennial. The early leaves of established perennials are more desirable.

The freshly cut leaves are used primarily in mixed or tossed salad. The fresh or dried excess leaves and stems are usually vinegared.

CELERY SEED
(*Apium Graveolens*)

Part Used: Stalks and leaves, seeds.

Celery is an excellent source of vitamins A, C, and B factors, and minerals of sodium, potassium, calcium, phosphorus, magnesium and iron.

Always eat this food uncooked.

Celery plants may be "borrowed" from the garden in the fall and stored in the cellar. Properly rooted in moist, rich soil, they will continue all winter to produce tender shoots for food and flavor.

The seeds are collected from the second year's growth and should be dried quickly and stored in a glass jar. Medicinally, celery seeds have been held in high repute as a "nerve sedative" and the records of the past 250 years give evidence that "they are of a warm carminative nature, dispensing wind in the stomach and bowels."

Celery leaves and seeds are used in cheese, sardine sandwiches, onion soups and chowder, and warm vegetable salads.

For nervous headache take celery seed, 1 part; catnip herb, 2 parts; scullcap herb, 3 parts, and make a warm tisane to be drunk every four hours.

CHERVIL
(Anthriscus Cerefolium)

Part Used: Leaves.

Its name is the corruption of its Latin counterpart, *cerefolium,* which may be literally translated: "The leaf of Ceres." *Cerefolium* is derived from the Greek word, *chaerophyllum*. *Chaero* means joy-giving, and *phyllum* means leaves. Its unusual taste has been reported to range from anise to tarragon.

Chervil resembles parsley in growth habits, and grows to a full height of some 10–15 inches—but prefers close company and the semi-shade of tall plants, so that it will be protected from the hot sun which may cause it to become rather bitter.

Cutting the leaves when seven or eight inches high will afford several "joy-giving" salads during the period. A new crop may be obtained in the fall if the herb is allowed to reseed itself. In addition, it is one of the last herbs to give a green crop late in fall and the first in spring.

Always eat this valuable herb uncooked. The roots of the early plants may be eaten raw like carrots, or later steamed quickly in as little water possible. Chervil combines well with all foods, vegetables, proteins and starches. It is best served with cold vegetable plate, or may be diced and mixed with cottage or cream cheese, steamed beets or cooked spinach. Sprinkle onto soup and egg dishes when served.

CORIANDER
(*Coriandrum Sativum*)

Part Used: Ripe seeds. The leaves.

Coriander, an annual, is grown chiefly for its seeds and does well in ordinary garden soil. Plants grow to a height of two feet. It is an easy self-sower. The seeds are gathered when near ripe, in about ninety days, the tops being cut and dried by suspension.

Use to flavor cookies, and Danish pastry. Use as an anise or caraway substitute; as a substitute for sage in meat loaf and stews, baked apple and pear.

Use the seeds as an ingredient of curry powder.

The ground leaves may be mixed with the honey and chopped onions of a recipe for sweet and sour meat-balls. The leaves are also added to bean and barley soups for extra flavor.

Continental Europeans have long recommended coriander and barley water as a mild aromatic, tonic-stimulant for convalescents young or old who cannot ingest solid foods.

COSTMARY
(*Chrysanthemum Balsamita*)

Synonym: Bible Leaf.
Part Used: Leaves.

This herb is today employed mainly as a tea substitute or tisane. It must be used most sparingly when flavor is needed for poultry or meat.

It has an agreeable spearmint odor though a bitterish flavor.

Costmary is best cultivated by crown and root division. The

leaves are first gathered in mid-summer, when plant is in full bloom, about three feet high, and dried in a sunless area.

Centuries ago, costmary and lavender were included in sachets and potpourris as a moth and insect repellent, "to lye upon the toppes of beds, presses, etc., for the sweet sent and savour it casteth."

BLUE HYSSOP
(Hyssopus Officinalis)

Part Used: Upper half of herb.

Blue hyssop is a bushy hardy perennial growing to a height of 2–3 feet and is so named because of its deep blue blossoms. Root cuttings will offer a yield of leaves within six weeks.

The freshly minced leaves and flowering tops are especially suited to flavor fruits, fruit cocktails, and pies. It may be substituted for mint in poultry, lamb or fish.

Medicinally, it is an effective gargle used with sage for sore throat or quinsy. A warm tea is beneficial to relieve the spasms of bronchial or asthmatic cough.

LOVAGE
(Levisticum Officinale)

Part Used: Leaves, stalks, roots.

Since its flavor and odor are so similar to but at least three times as strong as that of celery, lovage leaves and stalks may well make a less expensive substitute for celery seed whenever the latter's flavor is desired.

Young seedlings five to six inches high are transplanted outdoors in May about a foot apart. Mulch during summer with vegetable matter and stones to insure proper retention of moisture for root system. Protect against winter-kill with a heavy mulch of leaves.

Collect the tender leaves and use in summer vegetable salad and the stalks or roots for soups. Use the roots, too, in your herb vinegar.

The pungent and aromatic roots tend to act as a stimulant, diuretic and carminative.

Asthmatics will profit well by the daily doses of garlic followed by a warm tea of lovage root.

MARIGOLD
(Calendula Officinalis)

Synonym: Calendula, Garden Marigold.
Part Used: Flower heads. Florets.

Seeds are sown in ordinary soil in spring.

Marigold was common years ago in almost every garden and used principally as a medicine and dye. Today it is grown in flower gardens as a mere ornament and its benefits ignored.

A solution from the flowers was recommended by the old writers as an eye drop for "red and watery eies" and would "cease the inflammation and taketh away pain." A syrup of the flowers was said to "cure the trembling heart."

The petals were once churned with the cream to dye the butter yellow. Today they are an acceptable substitute for expensive saffron in preparing rice.

Calendula Cream today is manufactured by Otis Clapp as a healing salve.

The dried flower heads may be used sparingly in soup, stews and chowder while the petals (one teaspoonful) may be added to rubbing alcohol (two ounces) as an external application to cuts and bruises. As a cosmetic, astringent and "skin cleanser," the flower heads may be steeped in witch hazel extract or simmered gently in cold cream.

An effective healing ointment is made by boiling the flowers and leaves (tablespoonful) in unsalted lard (four ounces).

OREGANO
(Origanum Vulgare)

Synonym: Wild Marjoram.
Part Used: Leaves and flowering tops.

This perennial has been called pot marjoram, which botanically is identified as *Origanum onite*.

There is a marked difference of taste and aroma of plants grown in rich and in clayey soil, the latter condition being best for oregano.

Propagation is by simple root division in the fall, or by seed. The plant is not easily winter-killed if properly mulched.

Oil of Origanum contains a very large percentage of carvacrol. Because of its high camphor content, it is used medicinally for external and internal purposes: externally, in proprietary "germicides" and as a pain-relieving ingredient of liniments; internally, its carminative and diaphoretic properties are especially beneficial in indigestion, neuralgia and rheumatic conditions. A tisane of the herb will offer comparative effects.

Oregano is used in manner similar to marjoram.

The greater majority of Italian and French chefs prefer for most of their dishes, warm or cold, the seasoning quartet of basil, summer savory, thyme and oregano.

Macaroni or pizza requires a tomato sauce seasoned with oregano. It goes well with all tomato dishes, sauces, soups and as a vinegar in salads.

OSWEGO TEA
(Monarda Didyma)

Synonym: Bee Balm.
Part Used: Herb.

The Boston Tea Party was a protest against the unbearable taxes on imported tea. The patriots accepted three native substitutes for the China tea, choice number one being Oswego. The other two were Labrador tea (*Ledum palustre*) which was drunk by the patriots of the more northern states, and New Jersey tea (*Ceanothus americanus*) by those of the southern area. Any of these three is a real health drink, since neither contains caffeine or any other harmful ingredient.

Oswego tea is so called because herbalists and the Shakers who settled in the area of that New York city found the herb growing wild in the environs and soon began to pluck the leaves for their tisanes. The name bee balm obviously signifies the attention given to the nectar of this herb by the bees.

Oswego is easily propagated by plant divisions and enjoys partial shade and soil that is light and somewhat moist.

RUE
(*Ruta Graveolans*)

Part Used: Leaves.

This herb has of recent years gained some prominence as a source of a most worthwhile medicine called rutin. According to Prof. Heber W. Youngken, rutin "decreases capillary fragility and reduces the incidence of recurrent hemorrhage associated with a state of increased capillary fragility, in diabetic retinitis, pulmonary hemorrhages not caused by tuberculosis . . ." As for the uses of rue, Professor Youngken declares it to be a "calmative, in colic and atonic amenorrhea." Another herbal authority considers it "a bitter, aromatic stimulant, valuable in stomach cramps, hysteria and dizziness."

Similarly, we find that in colonial days an infusion or conserve of the tops of the young shoots were believed to be "good against the headache, nervous and hysteric disorders, weakness of the stomach and pains in the bowels."

Because of its intensely bitter taste when fully mature, the leaves were held effective to combat the Evil Eye.

Do use the herb sparingly in cottage or cream cheese, and salads of chicken, tuna and salmon.

Rue is not reliably winter hardy here in New England.

TARRAGON
(*Artemisia Dracunculus*)

Part Used: The leaves.

"Tarragon is not to be eaten alone in sallades, but joyned with other herbs as Lettuce, Purslain, and such like that it may also temper the coldnesse."

The usual method of propagation is by division of the root or crown in the spring, since the plant rarely produces fertile flowers. Don't worry about winter-protecting this herb. Unlike rue, it is quite winter hardy. It is best to change the site of the tarragon bed every three years to avoid disease.

To prepare tarragon vinegar, pick the leaves just before the plant flowers and let dry one day. The stems usually discarded in the fall should also be incorporated in a later preparation of herb vinegar. Pack in a wide mouth bottle and let stand ten days. Shake bottle every day. Strain and store in a cool place.

7

Wild Herbs

WILD ALLSPICE
(Lindera Benzoin)

Synonym: Spice Bush, Benjamin Bush.
Part Used: Leaves and fruits. Ground young twigs.

CULINARY USE   Use in vinegar and with pickled cucumbers. It provides a tea substitute (with mint) and a substitute for allspice.

The leaves and fruits of the wild allspice have been mixed with tansy flowers as a moth preventive; with ground sassafras bark as an insect repellent.

ANGELICA
(A. Atropurpurea)

Synonym: Archangel, Masterwort, Holy Ghost Root.
Part Used: Roots, stems, seeds, herb.

Many years before the white man set foot on the shores of North America, many Indian tribes had long considered angelica a reliable remedy for many ailments. The White Mountain Apaches, the Yavapai and the Tewa medicine men prescribed the roots for stomach disorders. For this purpose, a decoction of the coarsely ground roots was drunk warm, while in other instances the whole root was chewed. The Menomini prepared a hot plaster from the rhizome and roots, which was applied to the side of the body opposite the pain. This was a favorite medicinal plant of the Pah Utes. The root was bruised and employed as a poultice for pains and bruises. A tea made from the roots was used for pains in the stomach. To avoid catching a contagious disease, pieces of the root were placed in the nostrils.

Collect angelica as follows:

Roots—September, October.

Herb (above root) May to early July.

Seeds—June. Should be sown as soon as seed is ripe (August). For medicinal use, dry on cheesecloth rack ten to fifteen days.

Since roots are fleshy and very apt to be attacked by insects and mold, they should be dried quickly and conserved in air tight jars, with the added protection of a few drops of carbon tetrachloride or carbon disulphide. Will stay good for three to four years.

CULINARY USES   The stems are frequently cooked with rhubarb, prepared like asparagus or mixed into soups. The leaves may be included in soups and stews. Dried, ground and properly preserved in mason jars, they will provide excellent nourishment in fall and winter when "greens" are scarce. The roots and stems are candied, as with ginger, sweet flag, etc.

MEDICINAL USES   Angelica is a carminative, diaphoretic, stomachic, diuretic, and expectorant; it is useful in colds, coughs, rheumatism, and an excellent vehicle for nauseous bitter medicines.

BAYBERRY
(*Myrica Cerifera*)

Synonym: Wax Myrtle, Candleberry, Waxberry.
Part Used: Leaves. Berries. Dried bark of root.

True Bayberry (*M. Carolinensis*), the Southern species, possesses more wax and oil.

In the household, years ago, bayberry leaves were quite often substituted for the tropical bay leaves as a soup flavorer; while the fruits (berries) provided the early settlers with a most satisfactory aromatic wax to be cast into candle-forms.

Collect the bark, late fall. Wash root system thoroughly with cold water and separate bark by pounding with a mallet. When dried, preserve in well closed darkened containers. Collect the berries in early fall, when whitish gray. The leaves, mid-summer.

CULINARY USES Substitute for the imported bay leaf, and add the leaves and berries to soups and stews. Best method is to suspend them in cheese cloth (bouquet) and remove when through.

MEDICINAL USES The bark is most valuable as an astringent and stimulant in diarrhea and jaundice, and also, in the correction of liver disorders. A decoction of equal parts sumac, wild indigo, is used as a gargle and wash for inflammation of the throat and for tender bleeding gums. Externally, powdered bayberry is a mild stimulant to indolent ulcers and should be diluted with powdered elm bark (equal parts).

SWEET BIRCH
(*Betula Lenta*)

Synonym: Cherry-, Black Birch.
Part Used: Leaves and end twigs, collected in mid-summer.

CULINARY USES An ingredient in "native herb vinegar." Excellent after dinner drink or tea substitute. May be used in soups.

MEDICINAL USES Diaphoretic and stimulant to urinary organs. It is an excellent anti-rheumatic, because the oil of sweet birch yields the natural pain-relieving methyl salicyclate (also called oil of wintergreen).

I have found it recorded that "in 1861 after the Battle of Carricks Ford, the edible bark of Black Birch probably saved the lives of hundreds of Garnett's Confederate soldiers during their retreat to Monterey, Virginia. For a number of years after that, the route the soldiers took could be traced by the peeled Birch Trees."

The leaves of the White Birch (Betula Alba) are employed to mask disagreeable flavors of other medicines.

WILD CARROT
(*Daucus Carota*)

Synonym: Queen Anne's Lace, Bird's Nest.
Part Used: Root, seed, herb.

Collect root in late summer. Herb and seeds, upper half, before latter mature.

CULINARY USES   Seeds, in soups and stews, broiled or baked fish.

MEDICINAL USES   Root: stimulant and diuretic in kidney disorders.

Seeds: carminative and stimulant in flatulence, colic, and jaundice.

When taken internally it is a poison to threadworms, and a tea of this herb has long been used as a folk remedy for this condition. Until recently a preparation of the herb was sold in Europe under the trade name of Daucarysatum.

CATNIP
(*Nepeta Cataria*)

Synonym: Cat Mint.
Part Used: Leaves and flowering tops collected when in full bloom.

There is an old saying:

> If you set it, the cat will eat it,
> If you sow it, the cats don't know it.

The cultivator of catnip should never transplant any of the adolescent plants, for by so doing, he invites all the local felines to partake fiendishly of the immature crop. However, catnip grows easily from seed in sandy or rich, but not moist, soil, requires little attention, and assures one of an ample crop for several years. What appears so peculiarly and appreciatively pleasing to cats is the plant's volatile oil, similar in composition to that of valerian, which, too, produces the same stimulating, almost inebriating effect.

Superstition has it that chewing the root will make mild and gentle people quarrelsome and fierce, and there is an old English legend of a certain hangman "who could never screw up his courage to the point of hanging anyone until he had partaken of it."

CULINARY USES   Catnip is used today as a bouquet by many herb-minded folk, to flavor certain sauces and soups.

MEDICINAL USES   Carminative, diaphoretic, and antispasmodic.

The U.S. Dispensatory states this herb is efficacious in "infantile colic . . . used as a sudorific in colds and febrile complaints and in painful menses . . . chewing the leaves is reputed to relieve toothache."

It must be remembered, too, that as the drugstore elixir of catnip and fennel is bought by a worried mother to relieve her colicky infant, a warm infusion of catnip and fennel seeds, equal portions, will in most cases do the same.

In feverish colds, to induce profuse sweating, one part each of catnip, boneset, peppermint and one half of sage should be infused and drunk warm.

It has long been reputed to be of service in scarlet fever and measles when combined in equal parts with the orange-red saffron stigmas; and for a nervousness insomnia and nervous headache, with valerian root, scullcap and nerve root, one part each, as warm infusion; and to relieve toothache, with ground hops and sassafras bark.

A mixture of equal portions of catnip, anise, fennel and spearmint is of service as a carminative and as a tea or coffee substitute for the dyspeptic individual. Catnip (alone or in combination) should always be infused and covered until ready to drink to retain the volatile properties.

SWEET FLAG
(*Acorus Calamus*)

Synonym: Sweet Root, Sweet Cinnamon.
Part used: Roots and young shoots collected in spring. Leaves —spring to summer collection.

CULINARY USES To flavor fish and meat. Considered a good substitute for many of the foreign spices, as ginger, clove, cinnamon.

The roots are candied like ginger, angelica or lovage.

WILD GARLIC
(*Allium Canadense*)

Part Used: Top, bulbs, and stems.

Separate a whole garlic into the respective cloves (some 6 to 8) and plant in rich well-drained soil, or in such soil as is adapted for the growing of onions. Soon enough, the scallion-like tops have grown 6 to 8 inches high, high enough to be cut, and are ready to be collected.

CULINARY USES Cut close to the original clove, about one inch above the bulb, and then you may use the green tops either as is, mixed with other greens as celery, lettuce or crisp uncooked spinach; or else you may incorporate them in with cole slaw, although I prefer the open tossed salad. In either case be sure to include cress, either water or garden cress, and parsley. In cold salads, these two, parsley and cress, will disguise quite effectively the possible odors of the garlic oil. Garlic is a basic ingredient in many recipes, especially those derived from French and Italian cuisine.

MEDICINAL USES One of the oldest uses for garlic has been in the preparation of a syrup for bronchial cough and spasms, especially in asthma.

The essential oils of garlic contain constituents that kill bacteria, protozoa, and even larger organisms like yeast cells and eggs of certain lower animals. Experimental use of these compounds is being made in hospitals, particularly in the treatment of suppurative wounds.

The following is taken from a news report:

"Biological chemists have discovered a new germ-killing chemical in the common Garlic, which is called Allicin. It not only attacks types of germs which can be vanquished by penicillin but also others which so far have proved themselves immune to penicillin. What Science has now discovered only goes to prove what a lot of people have suspected all along—that Garlic's penetrating, potent and persistent flavor and odor ought to influence germs just as surely as it does people—but in a different way.

"Allicin attacks one of the commonest of all germs—the staphylococci that are found in boils and carbuncles. Allicin acts upon germs in the same way that penicillin does—not by actually destroying them on contact like Iodine or Bichloride of Mercury, but by limiting the bacteria's ability for further growth. It helps destroy the germ's oxygen metabolism just as a person may smother to death. It takes 100 times as much Allicin from Garlic to fight the germs developed in boils as it does for penicillin. If that's all there were to it, scientists wouldn't be much interested. But the big point to remember is that the Garlic chemical's value lies in combating some of the germs that penicillin won't touch. Such a germ is bacillus paratyphoid A, which created a disease in man closely resembling typhoid fever."

Garlic should always be considered a most valuable medicinal —both as a preventive against possible disease and then as a curative—when needed. Daily doses will help to fight diseases of the nose and respiratory tract, and have been recommended for persons with high blood pressure. It has been much used as an asthma remedy, and as a worm syrup. Moreover, it is an excellent intestinal antiseptic and an especially good stimulant to the digestive system.

Garlic, like onion, leek and chives, offers an excellent source of Vitamin C, and a fair amount of Vitamins A, B and G. It abounds in minerals of sulfur, iron and calcium.

WILD GINGER
(Asarum Canadense)

Synonym: Canada Snakeroot. Indian Ginger.
Part used: Roots, collected in spring.

CULINARY USES   Ingredient in mixed pickling spices. Substitute for and candied like ginger.

MEDICINAL USES   Stomach bitter, diaphoretic, carminative.

SWEET GOLDENROD
(Solidago Odora)

Synonym: Anise-scented Goldenrod.
Part Used: Leaves and flowers, summer collected.

Another "beverage" plant that makes a suitable tea substitute in the sweet goldenrod. Don't let the mention of goldenrod bring uncomfortable memories of being afflicted with hay fever.

The species to collect is the sweet or anise-scented goldenrod, one of the few of the fifty members of its family which yields a warm aromatic anise-like taste. This property is invaluable in disguising such bitter-tasting herbs as thoroughwort and verbena, and this trio is effective as an "old reliable" cold remedy. When you have identified this proper goldenrod, collect the leaves when the plant is in bloom and use them fresh or dried, with peppermint leaves, as an after-dinner summer tea (tisane).

Flowers will yield a yellow dye and may also be included in scent bags (sachets).

HORSERADISH
(*Armoracia Lapathifolia*)

Part Used: Leaves and root. Any excess of roots may be preserved for future use by covering in sand.

CULINARY USES   Use leaves as a potherb. Freshly ground root as condiment, served with fish or meats.

To prepare fresh white horseradish sauce, wash the root clean and let soak in cold water 2 hours. Grate root into enough vinegar to make sauce. To redden sauce, add grated beets or beet juice.

MEDICINAL USES   It is indicated as a stomachic, stimulant to digestion, diuretic and antiscorbutic.

The "5 bitter herbs" said to have been eaten by the Hebrews during their 8 days of Passover are horseradish, or wild radish (*Raphanos agrios*), coriander, horehound, lettuce and nettle.

Horseradish root is rich in Vitamin C, yielding 100 units, and proportionately that's more than lettuce and green peppers can boast of.

JUNIPER
(*J. Communis*)

Part Used: Dried ripe berries. Collected in August-September.

CULINARY USES   With game or meats, especially ham. Soups or stews, and sauce— use 5 or 6 berries to each preparation. Native spice vinegar—30 berries to each pint of vinegar.

May be used with savory, thyme and marjoram.

MEDICINAL USES   A stimulant diuretic especially indicated in cystitis. Must always be used in combination with other diuretics and demulcents. Also a carminative and stimulant.

MELILOT
(*Melilotus Officinalis*)

Synonym: Sweet Lucerne, Yellow Clover.

CULINARY USES   Potherb in soups and stews. Tisane with mint or balm. Tea substitute.

MEDICINAL USES   Emollient and mild aromatic.

GARDEN NASTURTIUM
(*Trapaeolum Majus*)

Synonym: Indian Cress.
Part Used: Upper half. Unripened seeds.

The common garden nasturtium provides a fair substitute for watercress and both the young leaves and the flower petals produce most pleasing effect in an otherwise dull salad.

The leaves and stems and especially the half-ripened seeds are often added to the jar containing pickles and allowed to remain a few days, later to be mixed with warm or cold salads.

Considered a delicacy by the Chinese.

COW PARSNIP
(*Heracleum Lanatum*)

Synonym: Masterwort.
Part Used: Collect leaf stalks and stems just before flowers expand. Seeds, before maturing. Root, early summer.

CULINARY USES   Leaf stalks as salad ingredient, in soups and stews.

MEDICINAL USES   Seeds and root as stimulant in nervous disorders and as carminative. Has been used in treatment of epilepsy.

PEPPERMINT
(*Mentha Piperita*)

Synonym: American-, Brandy-, Lamb-Mint.

Part Used: Dried leaves and flowering tops, collected before blooming of flowers. There may be two more cuttings.

Peppermint and all other mints are of very easy culture and are propagated by root cuttings.

HISTORY   The Russians today employ the very same therapy for a sore throat as used to be employed by Indian priests 2,000 years ago—inhalation of peppermint tea vapor.

Persian scripts dated at around 1600 B.C. contain several quotations on mint. The first of these scripts originates from Abu Mansur Mowafik who was a physician and wrote a pharmacological textbook. Two other Persian scripts make mention of mint as well and comment on its therapeutic properties. The script by Abu Mansur Mowafik lists the various therapeuticals and gives their indications. According to the somewhat peculiar medical conceptions of the ancient Persians, the author stresses mint to be a "hot and dry remedy." The indications are rather numerous. Mint is recommended as an expectorant, for monthly pains, against short-windedness. It is considered of value for removing tape-worms. It is expected to cure jaundice by opening liver obstructions. For sciatica, a compound of mint and honey is plastered onto the thigh. The deeply situated affliction is thereby "pulled outwardly" and the joints are warmed. Leprosy is supposed to be favorably influenced by peppermint cooked in wine. These are but a fraction of the indications mentioned in Mowafik's script. There is no doubt about mint having been the foremost therapeutic agent of the ancient Persian medical arsenal.

Osiander states in his textbook, *Popular Remedies,* 1838, that he found mint tea to be exceedingly valuable in the treatment of influenza. He used mint tea during the terrific grippe epidemics of 1833 and 1836 and placed its sweat producing effects far above the ones obtained from the lilac tea. He suggested that mint should be present in every garden. He stated that in his many years of practice he had been convinced that peppermint tea possessed a cramp subduing capacity. The chemical analysis of mint performed about 50 years later proved the correctness of this theory.

CULINARY USES   Use in jelly, fruit cup and drinks, potato and carrots, pea soup, with lamb or mutton.

Mint sauces can be quickly prepared, for use with fruits or desserts. Powdered or finely ground leaves are covered with boiling water, and allowed to stand (saucered) until cold. Mix with marmalade. Or take:

Herb (finely ground)	1 cup
Malt Vinegar	1 cup
Salt substitute	Pinch
Honey	2 ounces

The herb is mixed with the vinegar to which the salt has been added; the mixture is simmered ten minutes and allowed to stand covered about 30 minutes. Stir in the honey or enough to thicken to one's taste. Goes well with lamb or chicken.

MINT VINEGAR

Cider Vinegar	1 pint
Fresh Mint	1 to 2 cups
Brown Sugar	⅓ to ⅔ cup (optional)

Bring the vinegar to a boil, add the sugar and the washed herb. Stir well and simmer 10 minutes. Strain and immediately pour into hot sterilized bottles.

MEDICINAL USE   Diaphoretic, carminative, nerve stimulant and anti-spasmodic. Especially useful in colic, dyspepsia, nausea, and general bowel complaints, nervousness and headaches. For a nervous headache, drink a warm tea of sage, scullcap and peppermint every hour until relieved; to break a cold, hourly, even half hourly, warm drinks of peppermint, elder, boneset, sage and catnip are recommended.

As a carminative: catnip, dill and peppermint, equal parts for most stomach ailments. May be infused ten minutes and the tea drunk every ½ hour until relieved.

PEPPERGRASS
(Lepidium Virginicum)

Synonym: Cress, Land Cress, Bird's Pepper.

It was called cress because of its rapid growth, and derived from the Latin *crescere*, to grow.

Part Used: Young leaves, collected in spring. Seed pods, summer-autumn.

CULINARY USES   Its peppery flavor recommends its use in vegetable salads and cole slaw, and with soured cream and cucumber. Do not cook. Use dried powdered seeds as ingredient of salt substitutes.

MEDICINAL USES   To make a good hair "tonic": simmer a handful of ground herb (summer collected) in two pints of hot water for a half hour. Strain and add a small handful of finely ground sage leaves. Simmer another half hour. When cool, strain and add two ounces of bay rum.

SASSAFRAS
(S. Albidum, S. Variifolium)

Synonym: Wild Cinnamon Wood, Mitten Plant.
Part Used: Leaves, bark and pith (wood and bark for dye)

Sassafras is a shrub, 8 to 15 feet high, or a small tree, 20 to 40 feet high, quite common in New England and is usually called the "mitten plant" because one of its three kinds of leaves growing on the same tree is shaped like a mitten.

CULINARY USES   Spring collected leaves in potherb. Bark to season soup and stews, and ingredient of native spice vinegar. Makes a fine tea and powdered is used as a thickener for soups and gravies.

MEDICINAL USES   Bark in nearly all internal remedies; diuretic, anti-rheumatics, laxatives; "blood purifiers," and "spring tonics."

The name, sassafras, is a corruption of the Spanish word, *saxifrage* which, in turn, is derived from two Latin words *saxum,* meaning a rock, and *frango,* meaning "I break." That is why herbalists recommend to those sufferers with stones in the kidneys and other kidney diseases that sassafras be used. Other medicinal uses of the sassafras shrub include employing its spongy pith in combination with witch hazel leaves, as a very efficient eye lotion, while the bark and roots are included in a "blood purifying" formula.

To put sassafras leaves and bark to further use, combine the leaves with those of sweet fern for fragrant herb pillows; the powdered bark is a good ant powder.

A kidney stimulant is prepared by taking bearberry leaves, 4 parts; buchu leaves, 4 parts; corn silk, 2 parts; fennel seed, 4 parts; spearmint leaves, 2 parts; mallow leaves, 4 parts; doggrass (witchgrass) roots, 4 parts; sassafras bark, 4 parts, and steeping one teaspoonful of the mixture in a cup of hot water, covered with a saucer. When cool, stir, strain and drink entire cupful 4 times a day.

SHEEP'S SORREL
(*Rumex Acetosella*)

Synonym: Sour Grass.
Part Used: Fresh leaves.

CULINARY USES   Something different for that thick soup or puree or for cold salads or cole slaw.

SORREL SOUP   Wash sorrel and put in saucepan with a little water (not covered). Cook slowly for about ½ hour. Put four cups of milk with small white onion (whole) in double boiler, add two table-spoonfuls of butter plus two of flour to the hot milk. Let stand and add sorrel and strain. Season.

MEDICINAL USES   Diuretic and refrigerant. May be used as a cooling drink in feverish conditions.

Sheep's sorrel is a miniature form of the garden sorrel (*Rumex acetosa*) and like the latter is highly acid in taste and reaction. This very acidity is due to the acid oxalate of potassium and tartaric acid. These ingredients plus Vitamin C make it an important salad green.

This plant is not related to wood sorrel (*Oxalis acetosella*), trefoil or shamrock—though one may be substituted for the other as a culinary or medicinal.

SHEPHERD'S PURSE
(*Capsella Bursa-pastoris*)

Synonym: Lady's Purse, Pepper and Salt.
Part Used: Whole herb for medicinal purposes. Leaves, collected before flowering. Flowers and fruit.

When this herb matures, it produces flat seed-pouches which resemble an old-fashioned change purse—hence its familiar name. Be sure to collect many such plants and when they are completely dry, then strip the leaves and small fruit pods and preserve in sterilized, dry glass jars. These come in handy later in the fall and winter, and combined with peppergrass, add new zip and zest to a usually dull vegetable soup.

CULINARY USES   The young leaves are included in salads or cole slaw; the leaves and fruits, in soup.

MEDICINAL USES   Antiscorbutic, diuretic.

Its virtues are few but significant: when dried and infused, it yields a tea which is still considered by herbalists one of the best specifics for stopping hemorrhages of the stomach, lungs, uterus, and especially of the kidneys. Its hemostatic properties have long been known and are said to equal those of ergot and goldenseal. During World War I, the latter two drugs were unobtainable from European sources and were substituted by the fluid extract of shepherd's purse with excellent results.

Its antiscorbutic, stimulant and diuretic action caused it to be much used in kidney complaints and dropsy.

To make your own "styptic" solution, boil three ounces of herb in two pints of hot water. Internal dose is two teaspoonfuls every four hours. Externally, this solution, though liable to rapid fermentation, makes an excellent application for severe bleeding.

To make a healing ointment, simmer for a half hour one heaping tablespoonful of ground plantain and shepherd's purse leaves in 4 ounces of unsalted lard or mutton suet. Strain into ounce containers.

SPEARMINT
(Mentha Viridis)

Synonym: Garden, Lady's, Mackerel Mint.

Part used: Dried leaves and flowering tops, collected before blooming of flowers. Cut every 6 weeks thereafter.

CULTIVATION   Early in the spring, transplant a few roots to rich, moist soil in partial shade. To improve the mint bed, cut the leaves frequently and add plenty of water or add mulch leaf or mold around roots.

CULINARY USES   The powdered mint may be dusted upon gravies, soups and purees, especially pea and bean.

Mint sauce quickly prepared by adding the finely chopped herb to warmed vinegar, and syruped with sugar.

MEDICINAL USES   Substitute for peppermint.

TANSY
(*Tanacetum Vulgare*)

Synonym: Bitter-, Yellow Buttons.

Part used: Leaves collected in spring. Leaves and flowering tops, summer.

CULINARY USES   This plant will substitute for nutmeg and cinnamon.

MEDICINAL USES   Carminative, diaphoretic, anthelmintic, nervine.

OTHER USES   Equal portions of herbs of fleabane, pennyroyal and tansy (or their distilled oils diluted with alcohol) make a good mosquito repellent. An old time fly repellent recipe was composed of elder and tansy leaves.

Flowers' heads yield a yellow-red dye; the leaves, green.

NOTE   Must be used with caution, and always accompanied by other herbs. Centuries ago, herb tansy was rubbed onto and sprinkled over meats to preserve and protect them from flies and ants.

TREFOIL
(Oxalis Acetosella)

Synonym: Shamrock, Wood Sorrel.
Part Used: Upper half.

This weather-sensitive plant has been called the "husband-man's barometer" because it will completely shut up or double its leaves when a storm approaches but will fully unfold them in clear weather.

CULINARY USES   Adds distinctive tartness to cole slaw or salads, or to eat with soured cream or cheese. May be substituted for sorrel or cress species.

MEDICINAL USES   Refrigerant and diuretic. Drink only 2 cups a day of the tea, 4 when prepared with mint, either spearmint or peppermint.

WATERCRESS
(Nasturtium Officinale)

Synonym: Scurvy Grass.
Part Used: Leaves, collected in late spring, early summer.

This herb is a close relative of our common garden nasturtium, and is found growing abundantly in many of our native brooks. The tender young shoots have long been used as a salad green and as a garnish. Since ancient times watercress has been known as a food. "Xenophon recommended it to the Persians, in western India Cress was prized by the Mohammedans. The Romans considered it as the food for those who had deranged minds." Many people have bought this tasty green in markets at a high price but probably cannot recognize it growing in the brook in back of their own homes.

Watercress, sometimes called scurvy-grass, has long been relished by the old-timers who knew that no plate of salad vegetables was ever to be without watercress. This herb is quite tasty, as with other members of its family, having a definite peppery and slightly pungent flavor. Perhaps that is why it was called nasturtium, a name derived from two Latin words, the first *nasus* meaning nose and *tortus* meaning "turned up," because of its pungency.

CULINARY USES   Whenever possible include watercress in a Summer salad. Always eat uncooked.

MEDICINAL USES   An excellent anti-scorbutic and gentle stomachic and diuretic. Useful in skin and blood disorders, jaundice and kidney conditions.

Watercress is an excellent source of Vitamin C plus A, B, E and G. Its high Vitamin C content makes it an admirable food for the elderly since the vitamin will help maintain the suppleness of the small blood vessels and thus ward off hardening of the arteries. Watercress contains three times as much Vitamin C as the leaves of lettuce. Moreover, watercress may well boast of its content of health fortifying minerals as sodium, potassium and calcium, plus those that are constantly required to strengthen the blood stream, namely sulfur, iron and copper, and manganese. Watercress contains twice as much iron as spinach and four times that of lettuce.

WORMWOOD
(Artemesia Absinthium)

Synonym: Absinth, Mugwort.
Part Used: Upper half of flowering herb.

CULINARY USES   May be substituted for tarragon, but should be used with discretion. Formerly, wormwood was included in baking and roasting recipes. A small sprig may be placed beneath the meat or fish intended for one with general debility or weakened digestion following a prolonged cold or sickness.

MEDICINAL USES Stomachic and digestive tonic. Diaphoretic. It must be used with other herbs. Vinegar of wormwood gives almost immediate relief to bruises or sprains.

OTHER USES May be mixed with tansy or lavender to protect clothes from moths, fleas, and other insects.

References and Suggested Reading

Bankes, Richard. *Banckes Herbal,* London, 1525.

Bartram, T., Editor. *Health From Herbs,* Leicester, England.

Britton and Brown. *Illustrated Flora of the Northern States and Canada.*

Burr, Fearing. *Field and Garden Vegetables.*

Carque, Otto. *Vital Facts About Foods,* Natural Brands, Inc., Los Angeles, 1940.

Coles, William. *Nature's Paradise.*

Culpepper, Nicholas. *The English Physician,* 1826.

Esser, William L. *Dictionary of Foods,* John's Island, S. C., 1947.

Finck, H. T. *Food and Flavor.*

Foster, Gertrude B. *Herbgrower Magazine,* Falls Village, Conn.

Grieve, M. *Culinary Herbs and Condiments,* Harcourt, Brace & Co., New York, 1934.

Harris, Ben Charles.
   Eat the Weeds, Barre Publishers, Barre, Mass. 1969.
   Kitchen Medicines, Barre Publishers, 1968.

Hartshorne, Henry. *Household Cyclopedia.*

Henderson, W. A. *Modern Domestic Cookery.*

Herb Society of America. *The Herbarist.*

Hill, Sir John. *British Herbal.*

Holt, Rackham. *George Washington Carver,* Doubleday Doran Co., New York, 1943.

Hunter, Beatrice Trum. *The Natural Foods Cookbook,* Simon & Schuster, New York, 1961.

King, Eleanor Anthony. *Bible Plants for American Gardens,* Harper
& Bros., New York City, 1945.

Leyel, C. F. *Elixirs of Life,* Faber and Faber, London, 1948.

Lounsberry, Alice. *A Guide to the Trees,* Frederick A. Stokes Co.,
New York.

MacFadden, Bernarr. *Physical Culture Cookbook,* MacFadden Publications, Inc., New York, 1924.

Medsger, Oliver Perry. *Edible Wild Plants,* Macmillan Co., New
York, 1939.

Meyer, J. E. *The Herbalist,* Indiana Botanic Gardens, 1934.

Meyrick, William. *New Family Herbal.*

Perkinson, John. *Theatricum Botanicum,* 1640.

Reeder, David H. *Home Health Club,* Vol. 5, 1910.

Robbins, W. W. and Francis Ramaley. *Plants Useful to Man.*

Rohde, Eleanor Sinclair. *A Garden of Herbs,* Hale, Cushman and
Flint, Boston and New York, 1936.

Saunders, Charles F. *Useful Wild Plants of the United States and
Canada,* Robert M. McBride Co., New York, 1920.

Shelton, Herbert. *Hygienic Review,* Box 1277, San Antonio, Texas.

Stimpson, George. *A Book about the Bible,* Harper & Bros., New
York, N.Y., 1945.

Stratton, Robert. *Edible Wild Greens and Salads of Oklahoma,*
Oklahoma Agricultural and Mechanical College.

Turner, William. *Newe Herball.*

Walker, N. W. *Vegetable Juices,* Norwalk Press, St. George, Utah.

Wood, Horatio C. and Arthur Osol. *The Dispensatory of the United
States of America,* J. B. Lippincott Co., Philadelphia, 1943.

Yearbook of Agriculture, U.S. Department Agriculture, 1950–1951.

Youngken, Heber W. *Textbook of Pharmacognosy,* P. Blakiston's
Son and Co., Philadelphia, 1936.

Glossary

ALTERATIVE   An aid in re-establishing healthy functions of the body.

ANALGESIC   Helps to relieve pain.

ANTHELMINTIC   Has the power to destroy or expel intestinal worms.

ANTIBIOTIC   Restricts the action of or destroys organisms.

ANTICOLIC   Helps to prevent spasmodic pains in the stomach.

ANTISPASMODIC   Allays or prevents recurrence of spasms.

APERIENT   Gently laxates without purging.

AROMATIC   Used for flavoring, to make a remedy more palatable and to prevent griping.

ASTRINGENT   Has the property of contracting the tissue and arrests discharges or bleeding.

CARDIAC   Restores proper heart action.

CARMINATIVE   Expels gas from the bowels, stomach and intestines, overcoming colic and flatulence, and prevents the griping of laxatives or cathartics.

DECOCTION   The process of extracting plant principles by boiling herbs in hot water.

DEMULCENT   Soothes and protects the mucous membranes and allays the action of acrid or over-stimulating substances like laxatives.

DEOBSTRUENT   Relieves or removes obstruction to secretion or excretion.

DIAPHORETIC   Tends to increase perspiration by direct influences upon the sweat glands.

DIURETIC   Tends to increase the flow of urine and helps to improve or increase the elimination of the body waste products through the urine.

EMETIC   Causes vomiting.

EMOLLIENT   Has a palliative or soothing action.

EXPECTORANT   Facilitates the expulsion of mucous secretion (i.e., the phlegm of the bronchial passages).

FEBRIFUGE   Dispels fever.

HEMOSTATIC   Stops the flow of blood.

HEPATIC   Acts upon the liver.

INFUSION   The process of steeping herbs in boiling water, in order to extract its soluble principles.

NERVINE   Tends to quiet a temporary nervous irritation due to excitement, fatigue, strain or over-exertion.

PECTORAL   Helps to relieve afflictions of the chest.

REFRIGERANT   Has a cooling and refreshing effect on the body, helping to reduce slight fever.

SEDATIVE   Allays nervous irritability and exerts a soothing and quieting influence upon the nervous system, but has no narcotic effect.

STIMULANT   Said to gently increase functional activity. (Not in the category of artificial stimulants as tea and coffee, liquor, spices, smoking, etc.)

STOMACHIC   Promotes appetite and digestion by giving tone to the stomach.

SUDORIFIC   Greatly increases perspiration.

VERMIFUGE   Expels worms from the intestines.

VULNERARY   Helps to promote the healing of fresh cuts or wounds.

Appendix

SOURCES OF FRESH HERBS

Greene Herb Gardens, Greene, Rhode Island 02827

Little Compton Herb Nurseries, West Main Road, Box 526, Little Compton, Rhode Island

Meadowbrook Herb Gardens, Wyoming, Rhode Island 02898

Black Forest Botanicals, Route 1, Box 34, Yuba, Wis. 54672

Bittersweet Hill Nurseries, MD 424 & Governor's Bridge Road, Davidsonville, Md. 21035

Carroll Gardens, Box 310, Westminster, Md. 21157

Logee's Greenhouses, 55 North Street, Danielson, Conn. 06239

House Of Herbs, Salisbury, Conn.

Caprilands Herb Farm, Coventry, Conn. 06239

Hemlock Hill Herb Farm, Litchfield, Conn. 06759

A. Gilbertie Florists, Sylvan Road, Westport, Conn.

Frog Meadows Herb Farm, Washington Depot, Conn. 06794

Stonehedge Gardens, Box 257, RFD 1, Charlton, Mass.

Village Hill Nursery, Williamsburg, Mass.

The Herb Farm, Barnard Road, Granville, Mass. 01034

Mary Milligan, Corner Routes 110 and 111, Harvard, Mass.

Borchelt Herb Gardens, 474 Carriage Shop Road, East Falmouth, Mass. 02536

The Herbary, Homestead Road, Box 543, Orleans, Mass. 02653

Waynefield Herbs, 837 Cosgrove Street, Port Townsend, Wash. 98368

Cedarbrook Herb Farm, Rte. 1, Box 1047, Sequim, Wash. 98382

Merry Gardens, P.O. Box 595, Camden, Me. 04843

Pine Hills Herb Farm, Box 307, Roswell, Ga. 30075

Spring Hill Nurseries, 110 W. Elm Street, Tipp City, Ohio 45371

Sunnybrook Farms Nursery, 9448 Mayfield Road, Chesterland, Ohio 44026
John Wagner & Sons, Ivyland, Pa.
Forest Park Nursery, North Garden, Va. 22959
Taylor's Gardens, 2649 Stingle Avenue, Rosemead, Calif. 91770
Shirley Morgan, 2042 Encinal Avenue, Alameda, Calif. 94501
Hortica Gardens, P.O. Box 308, Placerville, Calif. 95667
The Herb Cottage, Washington Cathedral, Mt. St. Alban, Washington, D.C.
Shaker Maid Herbs, Box 2145, Idaho Station, Terra Haute, Indiana
Leodar Nurseries, 7206 Belvedere Road, West Palm Beach, Fla. 33406
Shuttle Hill Herb Shop, 256 B Delaware Avenue, Delmar, N.Y. 12054
Tool Shed Herb Farm, Turkey Hill Road, Salem Center, Purdy's Station, N.Y. 10578

SOURCES OF SEEDS

George W. Park Seed Co., P.O. Box 31, Greenwood, S.C. 29646
Joseph Harris Co., 36 Moreton Farm, Rochester, N.Y. 14624
Charles C. Hart Seed Co., Main and Hart Streets, Wethersfield, Conn. 06109
F.W. Bolgiane & Co., 411 New York Avenue, N.E., Washington, D.C. 20002

SOURCES OF DRIED HERBS

Cottage Herb Farm, 311 State Street, Albany, N.Y. 12210
Roth & Son, Importers, 1577 First Avenue, New York, N.Y. 10028
Norwalk Mills, 401 Grand Street, Brooklyn, N.Y. 11211
Atlas Importing Co., 1109 Second Avenue, New York, N.Y.
John Wagner & Sons, Ivyland, Pa. 18974
Penn Herb Co., 601 N. Second, Philadelphia, Pa.
Indiana Botanic Gardens, P.O. Box 5, Hammond, Indiana 46325
The Herb Cottage, Washington Cathedral, Mt. St. Alban, Washington, D.C. 20016
The Corner Cupboard, 591 Maple Street, Chatham, Mass.
Bushacres Herb Farm, Brandon, Vt. 05733
The Herbarium, Route 2, Box 620, Kenosha, Wis. 53140
Nature's Herb Co., 281 Ellis Street, San Francisco, Calif. 94102
Wunderlich-Dietz Corp., State Highway 17, Hasbrouck Heights, N.J. 07604

Index